## More Praise for *Dancing with the Diagnosis*

*Michelle beautifully describes the problems with a malignant disease from the patient's perspective, helping those of us in oncology better understand our patients' needs and improve our own communication skills.*

—James L. Poth, M.D.,
Hematology and Oncology, Dominican Hospital

*I was with Michelle during her treatment and witnessed firsthand what she did not only to cope with the illness, but also to take control and make something good out of something bad. She, in her own words, led the dance. The methods she used to help herself along the way are ones that we can all use, whether they are in context of dealing with an illness or other stressful events in our lives.*

—Stacey A. Starcher, R.N., B.S.N., M.P.A.,
Case Manager Hematology, Stanford University Hospital

*As a caregiver for someone who has successfully battled leukemia, I found the chapter on learning to be an active listener particularly useful. The sample dialogues aid the reader in understanding the importance of active listening when sorting through the negative feelings a cancer patient will experience. Michelle also provides a succinct and easily executed five-step approach to becoming an effective listener. I highly recommend this book for those embarking on the path to a successful fight against cancer and for those chosen to be a part of the support team.*

—Patrick McLane, Caregiver

Dancing with the Diagnosis *came along at the perfect time. I was in the middle of chemotherapy, feeling kind of alone. The book cheered me up in two ways. First, my ordeal was normalized because I got to observe someone else's "dance" with cancer. Second, I laughed out loud at some of the anecdotes! Humor is essential for healing!*

—Kristi Valentine, Leukemia Survivor

# *Dancing*

## with the DIAGNOSIS

### *Steps for Taking the Lead When Facing Cancer*

MICHELLE WATERS, M.A.

For Chuck—
Way to Go! This book looks so good... because of you!
Thank you for Everything!
Michelle

**Rising Star Press**
Scotts Valley, CA

Editor: Dr. Deanna L. Fassett

Interior design, composition, and copyediting by Joanne Shwed, Backspace Ink (www.backspaceink.com)

Cover and interior color pages design: Chuck Spidell, IllusioDesign (www.illusiodesign.com)

Original artwork for cover and interior pages: Kathryn L. Burton

Author photo: Liz DePuydt

**Library of Congress Cataloging-in-Publication Data**

Waters, Michelle.
Dancing with the diagnosis : steps for taking the lead when facing cancer / Michelle Waters.
p. cm.
ISBN 0-933670-10-9
1. Cancer--Diagnosis. I. Title.
RC270.W384 2003
362.196'994--dc22

2003018359

## ACKNOWLEDGEMENTS

My successful dance with cancer and the creation of this book would not have been possible without the love and support I received from many.

Thank you God for climbing this mountain with me and showing me what's possible. I continue to trust your plan for me!

Thank you Mom for not only giving me my wings, but for being the wind beneath them. You are so much more than my mother—you are my best friend and the most wonderfully influential person in my life. What an honor it is to be your daughter.

Thank you Brian, the Love of my life, for always making me feel like I am still your beautiful bride. You are so loving and you are so loved. Truly, together we can endure anything!

To Grandfather, my other favorite man: Through everything, you always made sure I never worried. I am so blessed to have you in my life.

Aunt Carol and Uncle Ray, thank you for opening your home to me and making me as comfortable as possible. I'm sending an extra big hug to you, Aunt Carol, for always anticipating exactly what I needed (from quiet time to homemade minestrone soup!) and for encouraging my book project from the very beginning.

Many thanks to Leslie, Sherri and Shannon. Whether it was the steady supply of ginger cookies, the coolest hospital room décor or the fabulous foot massages, I always felt supported by this circle of super sisters!

Thank you to the wonderful Waters family, Darrel, Jan and Tammy. From blood donations to caring cards, you took care of me like I was one of your own.

Hoshi, I always appreciated your optimism and great sense of humor. And you were right: It is now just a "blip" on the screen.

Thank you Suzi and Claire for feeding me a constant diet of inspiration and optimism.

And Emi, thank you for being you: perfect, positive and full of unconditional love.

I LOVE YOU ALL!

But wait . . . There's more!

I am forever grateful to the rest of my blood donors, both the ones I know (Linda, Laurie, Jim, Nancy, Leslie, Bob, Jack and Julia) and those who remained anonymous. A special thanks also goes out to my loving Crow's Nest restaurant family (led by Bob Munsey); and to Annie Rooke for taking such good care of Emi. Thank you Frank "Paco" Hannigan for bringing the first version of this project to life, and Jim Niland for carefully correcting an earlier draft.

To the Communication Studies Department at San Jose State University, thank you Dr. Dennis Jaehne, Department Chair, for encouraging me to teach and write; and Dr. Andrew Wood, for devoting so much time and energy to the creation of my website.

Thank you to Donna Jacobsen, publisher of Rising Star Press, for believing in my message. I'm also grateful for the fantastic team you pulled together to make this book a reality. A special thanks to Kathryn Burton for lending her wonderful original artwork to *Dancing with the Diagnosis*.

And, of course, I will always be thankful for the amazing medical professionals who guided my body into remission. They include Dr. Steven Coutre of Stanford University Hospital, Dr. James Poth of Dominican Hospital and Dr. Robert Baer of San Jose State University. To nurse Stacey Starcher: I wish everyone could have a case manager as outstanding as you.

T H A N K   Y O U   A L L !

To Macy,
the brightest star in my sky

## CONTENTS

# FOREWORD

Dear Reader:

Something drew you to this book. Perhaps it is your own diagnosis, or that of a friend. I want to congratulate you for making this excellent choice. By reading *Dancing with the Diagnosis,* you are beginning to take control of your circumstance. Strengthening your communication skills will strengthen YOU.

*Dancing with the Diagnosis* is not just another self-help book. This is an easy read for tough times. Practical, applicable exercises enable you and those you love to grow wiser and stronger as you face the challenges ahead. My own book, *Tough Times Never Last but Tough People Do,* highlights the power of perseverance and attitude through adverse situations. Michelle Waters echoes these principles while providing accessible information and uplifting testimony when the tough time is cancer.

At the Crystal Cathedral in 1998, Michelle inspired many as she read "The Dance" from her then-unpublished manuscript. Now that *Dancing with the Diagnosis* is available in local bookstores, I am thrilled to see that the power of her well-chosen words, positive spirit and unending faith has the potential for reaching so many more! Her professional background in combination with her own dance with cancer in 1997 make Michelle a credible and insightful "dance instructor."

Read. Dance. Lead.

In prayerful thoughts,
Dr. Robert H. Schuller

# The Dance

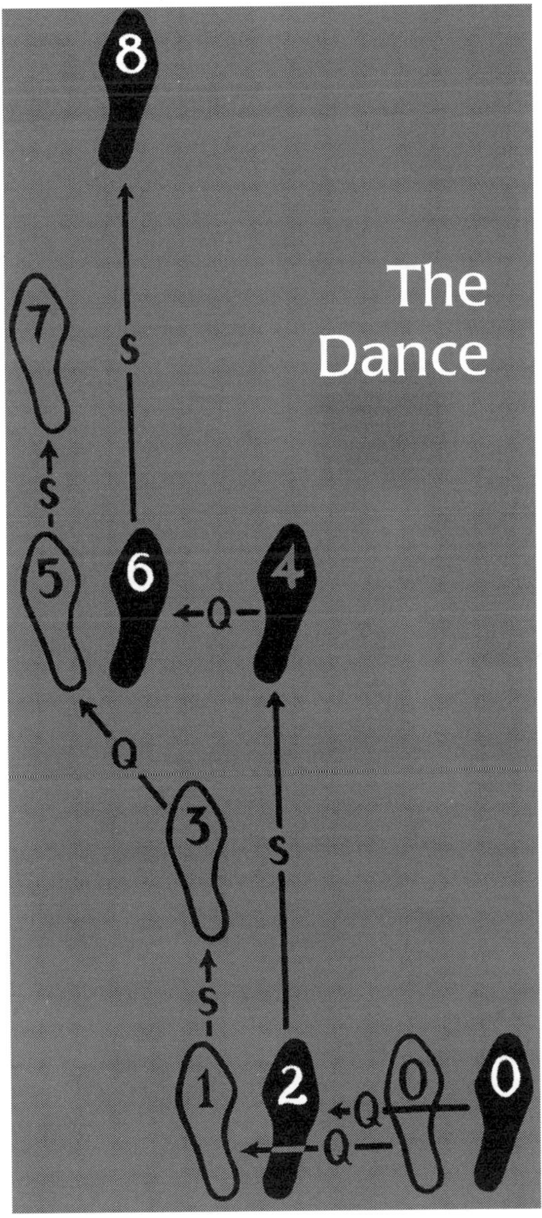

*"DANCE WITH ME," Cancer commanded.*

*"NO!" I shrieked in a fusion of fear and disbelief.*

*I wanted nothing to do with this would-be suitor and surely couldn't comprehend why he had chosen* me *in the first place. Before I could make sense of the insanity, I realized that this dance was not optional.*

*Cancer's clutch was firm as he led me to the floor. Arm in arm, we were clumsily stepping to the awkward beat of chaos. The dance he had choreographed for me was riddled with mismatched moves: dangerously low dips coupled with wild swings and unexpected turns. The music was equally discordant. High crescendos crashed into silence and the tempo wildly sped up again. Like a lifeless rag doll pinned to my partner, I was spun in circles of sadness until I was left physically and emotionally exhausted.*

*Just when I was sure I could dance no more, another dramatic change in tempo took me by surprise. My partner and I came face to face. Our eyes locked in fury. We seemed much less like dance partners now, but more like a matador and bull ready for the fight. (Looking back, I wonder, "*Which one was I?*") The new beat brought with it the realization that no longer need I follow in this twisted dance. If cancer and I were to be partners,* **I would lead**. *And lead I did!*

*My head cleared; my senses sharpened. Like water nourishing a wilted flower, control and determination rejuvenated every cell of my being. I kept my posture strong and my stride swift. My spirited steps were carefully planned, precise and perfectly timed with the new unfolding song. Our dance was transformed from one of a very physical nature to one created by the positive powers of my mind.*

*The distance between Cancer and me increased.*

*We were back to back, barely touching,*

*and it was not long until his shadowy figure was just a blur.*

*As the song faded into the past, I found myself dancing solo.*

*I stopped . . . caught my breath . . . and smiled.*

*I slowly exited the dance floor a wiser and more beautiful person.*

# Introduction: The Music Begins

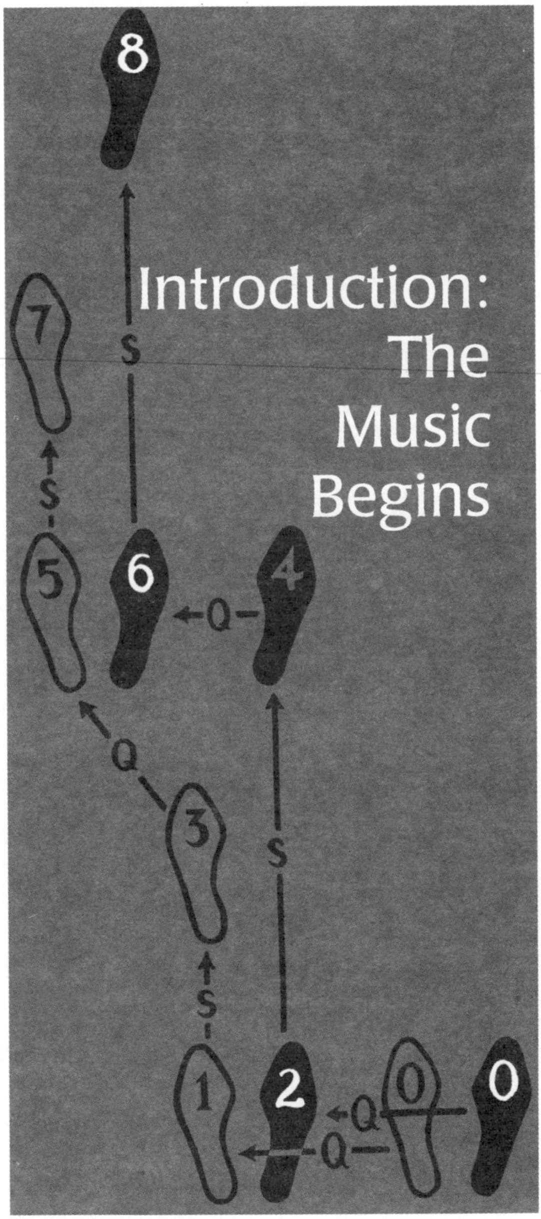

***My story, or how I came face to face with cancer, is unique.***

On February 26, 1997, my guardian angels were working overtime. For no other reason than because I had time to waste on campus, I decided to go for my annual health exam at San Jose State University, where I was a graduate student studying communication. During the routine exam, I requested a cholesterol test. My husband and I had a bet as to whose cholesterol was lower and I was determined to "win." Though I had not a single physical complaint and felt quite well, the blood test required for the cholesterol reading showed that my white blood cell count was extremely low and the alarmed nurse practitioner called my home to notify me. Two weeks later, on March 13, after seeing two specialists and eventually getting a bone-marrow biopsy ("just to get some answers"), my hematologist called me and apologized: I had been diagnosed with leukemia.

***My story is just like everyone else's.***

After receiving the news, I was speechless. I sobbed. My husband shouted. My mother cried. My family, friends and I now shared something new: shock, disbelief and fear. My life, like any other person who has been diagnosed with a life-threatening disease, had changed forever in a millisecond.

As the word of my diagnosis spread, I was showered with support from loved ones. Many caring people sent me books . . . lots of books . . . books with the word "cancer" in the title. "When did I get into *that* category?" I questioned. "Since when did cancer books apply to *me*?"

Skimming the books, I became even more overwhelmed. As helpful as they may have been, there were *too many words* for me to comprehend at the time. I experienced an instantaneous information overload. I knew I needed less. I needed instructions, inspiration and advice in the form of *snippets.* I thought if I was overwhelmed, others must be, too. I then started to write about my own process of healing, learning and adapting as I began to dance with my diagnosis.[1]

I offer this book to those of you who have been recently diagnosed with an eye-opening illness and, like me, need to avoid information overload. It also embraces some of the needs of your family and friends. Much of the information here is what helped me and my caregivers through some very hard times. I have been where you are now and I know that there are ways for you to make things better.

Provided here are short, accessible chapters with examples, options, suggestions and activities concerning you and your newly changed life. Topics range from communicating with physicians and shifting perspectives, to permitting anger and successfully surviving the shock of hair loss. Most chapters have a common theme of communication, self-acceptance and control. The experience of reading this book is meant to be active rather than passive. Included are several activities that enable you to practice and personalize the suggested lessons. In a journal-like fashion, there is space at the end of each chapter so that you can jot down your thoughts and reflections along

1. Most of this book was written while I faced treatments, hospitalization and shaky prognoses. I have been there, done that. I "get it."

the way. It is my wish that you find hope, humor, miracles and gentle doses of reality within these pages.

One of the most frustrating things about disease is the utter lack of control one feels after hearing "the news." In many ways, we are no longer in control of our bodies or our lives (at least as we knew them). For me, regaining some sense of control was crucial to my sanity, survival and fight against the disease. Communication and self-acceptance were the keys to the control I sought. Along those lines, this book presents simple and concise empowerment techniques for those who feel powerless. It reveals choices for those who feel choiceless.

I will ask you to make one choice before reading any further: **Choose to open yourself to the option of seeing things differently.** Despite what you may have heard, cancer is NOT a death sentence. *No matter what the prognosis,* I see cancer as a sentence for us to live life like we've never lived it before, making important changes in attitude and action along the way. Shocking as it may sound, whether or not we survive the disease is not as important as how we live life from this moment forward. This is one trip in which the journey is truly more important than the destination. Our diagnosis powerfully signals us that it is time to heal, time to learn and time to teach.

While reading these pages I invite you to devour what you like and spit out what you don't. Sometimes you may want to hold the words close to your heart and, at other times, you might want to throw the book across the room. *Do it!* The point is that the choice is yours. You are in control now. I know you did not choose this illness. Now I want to illuminate the many choices you do have through your healing process. Always remember that you are not your diagnosis,[2] but so much more!

2. I often use the word "diagnosis" in place of the word "disease" for the following reasons. First, the word "diagnosis" indicates a conclusion the doctors have reached. It may be *in us*, but it is not *of us*. On the other hand, "disease" is an emotionally charged word that becomes descriptive of something we physically "have" (e.g., "I *have* cancer"). The conscious choice to use (or not use) these words does not deny our medical condition. Instead, it serves to semantically separate the illness from who we are. See Lesson 1, "Choose Your Words Wisely," for a continued discussion of this principle.

# Shift Your Focu

It is time to shift your focus away from the diagnosis and onto your healing process.

LESSON

# 1

# Choose Your Words Wisely

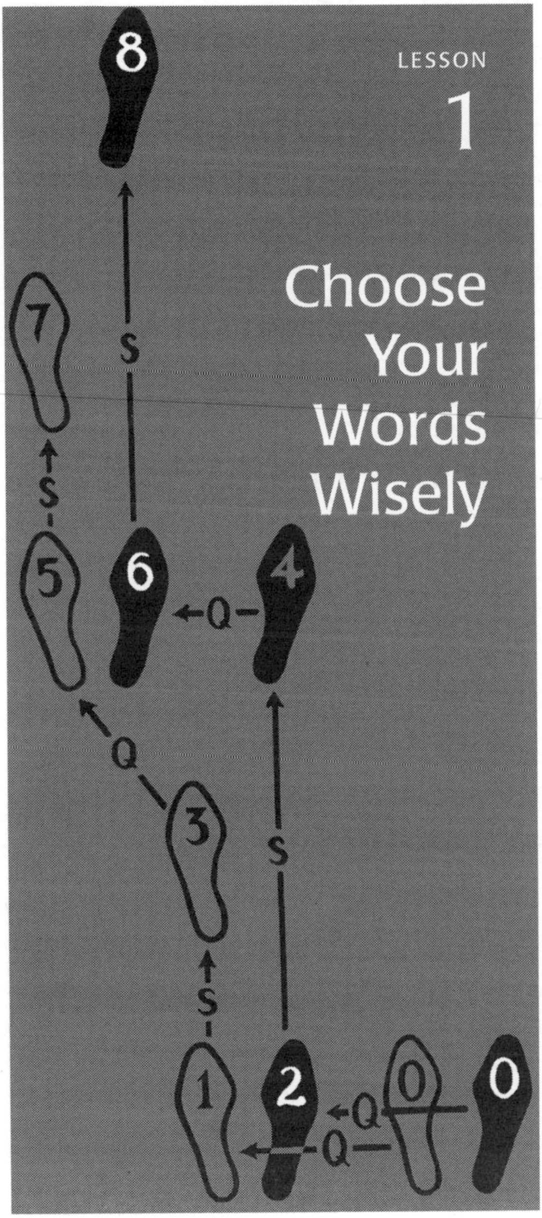

We did not choose our health issues. We did not ask for our lives to be put on hold. We did not volunteer for repeated hospital visits. We did not choose to dance this dance! When we reluctantly start our dance with a diagnosis, decision making feels out of reach and personal control is seemingly lost. As we search to regain our personal power, it is essential to first review and perhaps modify the words we choose.

Shortly after my first chemotherapy treatment, I was watching a morning TV news program that featured a remarkable teen who had just battled cancer . . . and won! I was shocked to see the caption "Cancer Victim" printed beneath his name. *Cancer Victim*? Wasn't this an inspirational story about a *Cancer Victor*? I started to look at my own labels. From that moment on, I refused to be a cancer victim! Maybe a cancer **fighter** or a cancer **survivor**, but never a victim—no matter what my outcome. I knew that my word choices mattered.

While monitoring my words, I also refused to take ownership of the disease. From the beginning, I did everything possible to step around the general statement, "I have cancer." Those three words powerfully implied ownership of something I didn't want. Instead, I chose to say, "I have been diagnosed with . . . " or "I am facing some medical challenges . . . " or my personal favorite, "I am dealing with a little blood issue right now!" The point was not to trivialize or deny my experience, but to clearly depict cancer as something that was separate from *who I was.* It was not something I *had*; it was something I was *dealing with*. Simple semantics? Ultimately, I felt empowered by the words I used.

We are all empowered by the words we choose. You can choose *not* to be a victim. You can choose *not* to own the disease. This is first reflected through your word choices that later resonate through to the core of your being.

The cycle is significant: Our word choices shape the realities we see, and the realities we see are reflected in the words we choose. Figure skater Scott Hamilton, a victorious cancer survivor, also noted the power of language in a televised interview with Tom Snyder. Hamilton told how his doctor used the word "mass" instead of the word "tumor" when relaying the diagnosis of cancer to him. The beloved skater said that the word "mass" was less threatening and easier for him to handle. Despite the word choice, the bottom line was still the same: Scott Hamilton had been diagnosed with cancer. Still, the words used to talk about this diagnosis made a big difference in his ability to accept it.

Censoring the negative words that creep into our daily vocabulary is another way to exercise control of our word choices and, thus, our realities. For instance, I once told my mother that I dreaded Fridays—my clinic days—because I always seemed to get some sort of *bad news* from my doctors. For me this was true. My reality was that clinic days meant bad news. I had plenty of evidence to support this, as I always seemed to learn something I would have rather not known on Fridays.

Being the ever-wise woman that she is, my mom instantly picked up on my use of the word "bad." Why would anyone in their right mind look forward to a visit where they received something "bad" each time? From then on, she asked that I not use the word "bad" to describe the kind of news I received on Fridays. Instead, we would view news that wasn't immediately favorable as mere information; we would simply refer to such information as just plain "news." News of a more encouraging type (improved health, steady progress) would be labeled as "good news," and news that topped the others (no need to be admitted to the hospital, surprise improvements) would be called "amazing news."

After each clinic visit, I would classify that day's news and report back to my mom. Eliminating all possibilities of "bad" news from my mind and allowing myself to choose between neutral and positive alternatives softened the edge of many appointments.

Another example of the power associated with word choices is connected to the clauses "have to" and "get to." Please say the following two sentences out loud:

**I have to go to the hospital tomorrow.**
**I get to go to the hospital tomorrow.**

The first, "I have to," implies obligation. The second, "I get to," implies opportunity! Either way, the situation is the same. I am going to the hospital tomorrow, but now I have two very different ways of viewing the experience: one positive and one negative. Consider this: *I get to* go to the hospital because my doctors know what's best for me. *I get to* go to the hospital because I have insurance. *I get to* go to the hospital because I live in a country where this is an option: medical care is readily available and research is a priority. Here, perception is influenced by word choice.

My mother drove me particularly crazy with this exercise. Every time I slipped and gloomily said that I *had to* do something related to my health care, she'd beam, "No, Michelle, you *GET TO* do that!" (Trust me, she's the only person who could constantly get away with that!) Sometimes I would gratefully accept the empowering shift; other times I would furrow my brow, grind my teeth, and say, "Yes, Mother, I *get to* do that!" Deep inside, I'd still acknowledge the positive difference that my choice of words made.

Substituting the clause "I CHOOSE TO" has a similar effect. Used with the example above, saying, "I choose to go to the hospital tomorrow" frames a different picture. Sure, going to the hospital may not top my list of things I want to do tomorrow, but by accepting my role in my healing process, I have agreed to do what is necessary for my body. Essentially, I have chosen this route of treatment and my words reflect such choices. You too can make a change for the better by choosing your words wisely. What we say shapes what we see.

**What Kind of News Did You Receive Today?**

AMAZING **TERRIFIC** WONDERFUL INTERESTING *GOOD*

**mediocre** AWESOME *INCREDIBLE* **BRILLIANT**

FANTASTIC INSPIRATIONAL ACCEPTABLE EDUCATIONAL

COOL **O.K.** SENSATIONAL **ENCOURAGING** GLORIOUS **EPIC**

MAGNIFICENT *SUPER* GREAT groovy *MARVELOUS*

delicious INFORMATIVE Motivating **STELLAR** just plain news

## KEY CONCEPTS: CHOOSE YOUR WORDS WISELY

- Choose your personal labels carefully. Be a cancer fighter or cancer survivor, but never a cancer victim!
- Do not own the disease.
- Eliminate the negatives from your vocabulary. They play no role in your healing and bury choices. Negatives include: can't, won't, should, must and never.
- Replace the clause "I have to" with "I GET TO" or "I CHOOSE TO" for quick, positive perspective shifts.
- Keep in mind that what we say shapes what we see.

## PUT IT TO PRACTICE

1. Monitor your word choices for 24 hours. Be on the lookout for have-to's, should's and must's along with any other words that might best be replaced by more empowering language.

2. After identifying limiting speech patterns, try substituting healthier words for those that are not serving you. Ask a close friend to help you with this. It is typically easier said than done because our communication patterns become ingrained and automatic. Be patient with yourself!

3. Note any changes that your new word choices make for you. Remember that words won't change the events in your life, but they can change your perception of those events.

## *Thoughts and Notes*

*"Change your thoughts, change your world."*
*—Norman Vincent Peale*

LESSON

# 2

# Gain Power Through Perspective

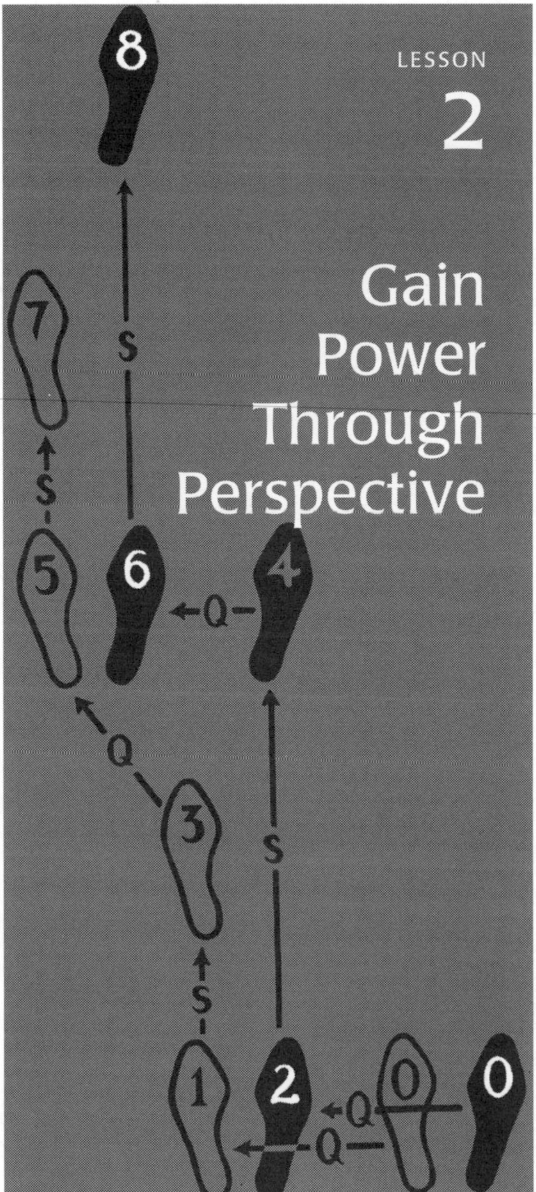

The old, rhetorical question "Is the glass half full or is it half empty?" is often used to determine optimism and pessimism, and at its root is the power of perspective. Perspective is the vantage point from which we choose to make sense of our situations and surroundings. It offers us one more area where we can make powerful choices and maintain control as we face cancer. Just as we empower ourselves and change our experiences through the words we choose, we can also do so through consciously selecting our perspective.

The natural division in perspective lies between seeing things as either positive or negative, although it's essential to realize that there are always many other options in between. Some people may see this dance with the diagnosis as a curse; others will see it as a blessing; still others will see it as a lesson. People may view disease as the worst thing that has ever happened to them; others may see it as the best; still others may chalk it up as another one of life's challenges. None of these people is right or wrong. Like patrons admiring a painting in a museum, they are standing in different spots of the room, interpreting their situation from different frames of reference. Perspectives, and the perceptions that follow, are subjective.

Perspectives initially stem from our belief systems. Think of your belief system as a prism: you receive information, it beams through your belief system and is then refracted accordingly. People who "look at the world through rose-colored glasses" and believe that "every cloud has a silver lining" are living lives guided by positive prisms and, therefore, perceive their circumstances in such a light. Those whose life's creed is "the grass is always greener on the other side" or Murphy's Law (if anything bad can happen, it will) experience life very differently than their optimistic counterparts. Whether they know it or not, both are making choices as to how they will interpret life's events.

Because they stem from our beliefs, we often assume that our perspectives are inherent. We say that we see things in a certain light because that's just "who we are" or "how we were raised." While it is true that certain points of view may become habitual, perspective is always a choice. Really. Let me say it again: **Perspective is always a choice.** We always have the choice to shift positions in the museum, so to speak, and look at our situations from different perspectives, angles or viewpoints. So often we don't acknowledge this or we never take the time to move.

The belief I have chosen to guide most of my interpretations is that everything happens for a reason, and that reason is usually a good one—even if it isn't revealed for quite some time. Sure, you may have heard that before (at least the first part), but try that perspective on for a minute. If everything happens for a reason, then nothing "just happens." If the reasons for which everything happens are usually good, then I am forced to look for the positive. From this perspective, I can attribute purpose and value to every event that life hands me. For me, this is a powerful vantage point! It allows me to extract good from *every situation,* no matter how big or small, pleasant or unpleasant. From this perspective, I can also practice patience, knowing that I am not always privy to the big picture.

Still, sometimes I forget this. For example, I had a rare allergic reaction during my first blood transfusion that left me very frightened.

I broke out in hives and, worse yet, my throat began to close, making it nearly impossible to breathe. Thankfully, an amazing nurse, Nettie, calmly yet swiftly took control of the scary situation.

As all of this happened, a whirlwind of negative thoughts spun through my mind. (This was not coincidental. Negativity typically stems from fear.) I was angry that my body was rejecting the blood products upon which my life so desperately depended. Knowing little about transfusions, I frantically wondered if this meant that I could receive no blood products in the future. I was mad that something supposedly "rare" was happening to me. I didn't want to be rare. I wanted to be run-of-the-mill predictable! In the midst of this mental mayhem, a small voice whispered, *"Everything happens for a reason, Michelle."* Oh yes! I had forgotten.

When things settled down, I learned that people like me who have allergic reactions to blood products may still, indeed, get transfusions; we just require special filters—and with those filters, by the way, comes a lot of extra attention. In large print, my medical charts now blurted, "THIS PATIENT HAS SPECIAL NEEDS."

Each time I was at the hospital, the nurses paid much closer attention to my transfusion process. Hmmm . . . I liked that! Whether routine or not, I would prefer special filters and premium care anyway. My perception of what could have been seen by many (including me) as a big hassle had shifted. From the initial vantage point of fear, I had moved to a place where I viewed the entire situation as something for which to be thankful. Ultimately, my chosen positive prism won over my initial fear-based reactions.

Just as changing our words changes our realities and vice versa (Lesson 1), so does changing our perspectives. It's all connected.

Another powerful lesson in perspective took place when my mother and I were waiting outside of the hospital for a prescription to be filled. We were exhausted and irritable. As we sat on a large concrete slab, four six-year-olds began to joyfully chase each other in circles. They were extremely close to us and one of them almost stepped on my mom.

"Watch out!" they exclaimed with joy.

"*You* watch out!" my mother replied. The last thing we needed were rambunctious kids! Then something wonderful happened. Noting their continuous round-and-round behavior, my mom somewhat sarcastically said to me, "I wonder what would happen if they changed directions."

"Change directions," I said dryly, loud enough for the children to hear. And they did.

"Change directions!" my mom repeated, amused that they had listened.

And they changed directions again. Now the children weren't the only ones who were smiling. My mom and I were, too!

"Moo like cows!" I teased.

"*Moo! Moo!*" they chorused.

"Bark like dogs!" my mother added.

"*Woof! Woof!*" they chimed.

The children were having fun and so were we! The playful interactions went on for some time. We may have been tired, but they were tireless. Soon we all introduced ourselves, and my mom and I learned that three of the four were triplets. They were waiting outside with their uncle while their grandmother finished with her clinic appointment.

At first glance, they looked like average six year olds, but my mom and I knew better. They were actually teachers of love in disguise. We continued to guide their play with silly commands until my prescription was ready. A simple change in perspective—making a choice to embrace these children and their energy instead of shunning them—made a wonderful difference in our day.

As demonstrated, life's events are subjective, meaning that any one experience is open to many varied interpretations. Human perceptions are never cast in stone and may change often. Think of your early childhood perception of kissing . . . YYUUCCKK! Now think of your adult view of kissing . . . *mmm* . . . See what I mean? Perception shifts happen first when we accept the fact that we have the option to see things differently and, second, when we seek out those perspectives that will influence favorable interpretations.

In *Chicken Soup for the Surviving Soul,* an anonymous poet lists the incredible things over which cancer is powerless. It cannot, for example, suppress memories or shatter hope. I challenged myself to list the powerful, yet positive, things that cancer *can* do. Here's what I came up with:

Cancer can:

- jump start life
- teach love

- strengthen the soul
- open eyes
- deepen relationships
- unmask miracles
- bring me back to myself

I challenge you to shift your perspective in an area related to your health where you see only the negative. You might choose to write your own positive "Cancer Can" or "Cancer Can't" poem. Perhaps it is possible to see cold, distant doctors instead as busy, dedicated professionals. Maybe you could reframe and see an overprotective and worried relative as a very concerned and loving caregiver. Same picture, different frame; same event, different perspective. Changing your perspective *does not* mean denying your original thoughts or feelings and it *does not* mean lying to yourself. It *does* mean looking at things in a more empowering way that you may not have originally considered. The mere acknowledgement of another perspective opens you up to infinite choices.

If shifting views is new for you, first try to detach and depersonalize that which you are trying to reframe. It isn't necessary that you jump immediately from the negative to the positive. Step outside the situation. Try to see it objectively without the emotional value you have attributed to it. Brainstorm a list of alternative ways to see the specific issue. For example, suppose the issue you wish to reframe is the diagnosis of the illness itself. Maybe you are having trouble seeing cancer as anything but an unfair cruelty of life. To reframe, you must detach. Ask yourself what fact is at the base of your present thought. In this case, it might be that "cancer is a life-threatening disease." Okay, that's true. From the original, emotionally charged negative thought of "cancer is an unfair cruelty of life," we have moved to a neutral, fact-based statement. Now there is time to think of positive ways to view the issue. For example, are there any benefits that a life-threatening illness can provide? Play along here . . . are there any you can think of? (Take a look back at the "Cancer Can" poem.)

For many of us, the diagnosis of a life-threatening illness gives us a chance to stop playing games or to see what's really important in life. With these new options and perspectives, we may now choose to reframe our original interpretation of cancer as something that is cruel and unfair, to something that gives us a chance to clarify our values and live life more appreciatively.

When exploring options, *try on* the new perspectives that come to mind. Don't just take a peek from this new place; instead, fully embody the fresh point of view. What does your situation look like from a different place of reference? What does it feel like here? What are you noticing that you hadn't noticed before? Are you comfortable here? Why or why not? Keep trying on new perspectives until you find the one that best fits your life.

If at first your new point of view feels phony, start smaller and practice in areas with which you aren't so emotionally involved. Maybe you could shift your perspective about the call-waiting telephone feature, and choose to see it not as an interrupting nuisance but as a practical bit of technology. You might choose to view the frustration of bumper-to-bumper traffic as a great opportunity to connect with others in the car or a chance to catch up on best-sellers by listening to books on tape. Bounce your ideas off a friend. Together, you can search for a happy medium between the two extremes. When you do finally make a shift from a perspective that is not serving you and your healing process to a better one, take note of the wonderful chain of events it sets into motion.

**Remember:** you can choose to see things differently. Choosing your perspectives is an empowering tool and it is one more area in which you can lead in this dance.

## KEY CONCEPTS: GAIN POWER THROUGH PERSPECTIVE

- You have many options to see things differently.
- How you interpret something—negatively, positively or anywhere in between—is ultimately up to you.
- A belief system (the base of perspective) is like a prism that refracts incoming information in positive or negative ways.
- Acknowledging new perspectives uncovers infinite choices and possibilities.
- Changing perspectives is easier when you first detach yourself from the issue at hand and then seek alternative points of view.
- Sometimes you must try on several perspectives before finding the one that best fits you and your circumstances.

## PUT IT TO PRACTICE

Take a topic, such as your career (whether it is inside or outside of the home/past or present), and look at it from each of the following perspectives, fully embodying each as you "try it on." One at a time, ask yourself what your career would look like if each statement were true.

1. It's a terrible waste of my time.

2. I am thankful to have learned so much from it.

3. It's depressing.

4. I am challenged by my work.

5. I am overwhelmed by my work.

6. I make a difference through what I do.

## *Thoughts and Notes*

*"The human spirit is stronger than anything that can happen to it."*
*–George C. Scott*

# LESSON 3

# Communicate Assertively

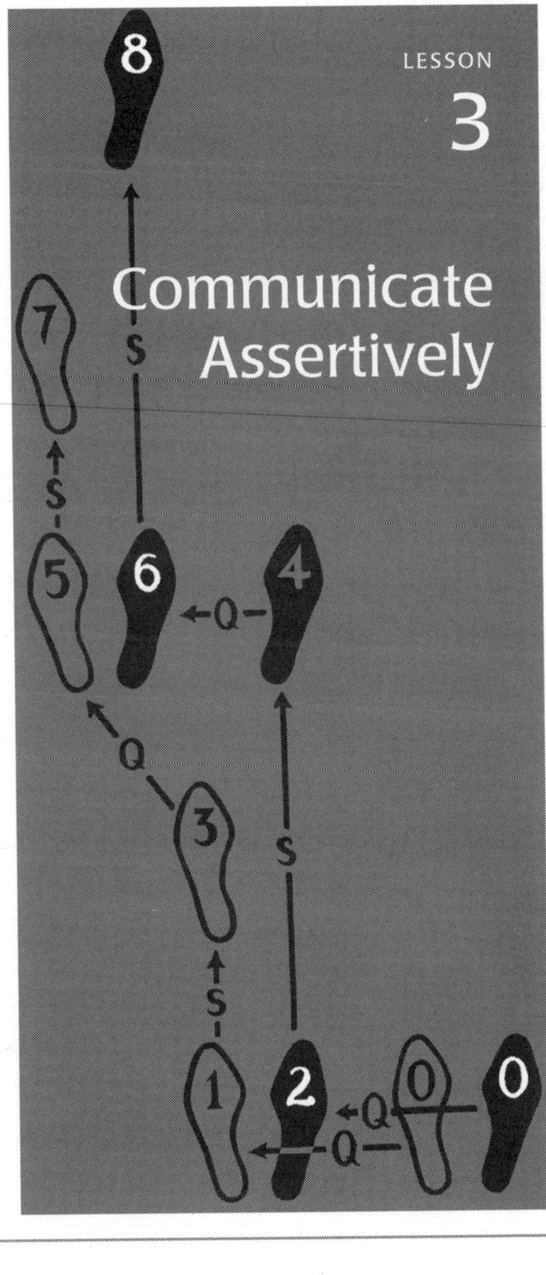

COMMUNICATION . . . a wonderful, though inescapable, part of being human. We communicate with our friends, our family members, our co-workers, our caregivers, our doctors and so on. Communication is a natural and essential part of our human existence. *We do it all the time.* Still, just because we do something often doesn't guarantee that we're good at it and, sometimes, there may be ways for us to improve upon our existing skill level.

Wait a minute. Is communication a *skill*? Is it really something that we can *learn*? My answer (particularly as a communication instructor) is a resounding ABSOLUTELY! And that's what this chapter is all about. Communication is an integral part of leading our dance with the diagnosis. Often it marks the difference between getting or forfeiting the control we seek. We already spend a great deal of time carefully considering the physical part of our health situation: We try to choose the best doctors and the best treatments. Now we need to focus on using the most effective communication options.

Sending responsible, assertive messages is one of the first steps toward communicating effectively. Assertive communication is the direct, open and honest approach of sharing ideas while respecting all parties involved in the interaction. When we communicate assertively, we acknowledge our own wants and needs while acknowledging the wants and needs of others. Instead of positioning ourselves on an unbalanced seesaw in a superior ("one-up") or inferior ("one-down") position to those with whom we are communicating, assertive communication requires that we enter the situation balanced and as equals.

Both aggressive and passive communication, on the other hand, involve an imbalance of status. When communicating aggressively, we assume a "one-up" power position that disrespects the needs of others. One who communicates aggressively may be seen as bossy, hotheaded or rude. Passive communication is the opposite: We place our interests below those of our co-communicator(s), putting ourselves in a "one-down" position. Essentially, we give up our power. One who communicates passively might be labeled as wimpy, wishy-washy or weak.

Consider these three different communication styles as they are applied to the following scenario: After my initial diagnosis, the supportive phone calls I received from family and friends really helped me maintain the hope and strength I needed. As I reflected on all those who had expressed their concern, I realized that I still hadn't heard from one of my co-workers, Julie. Julie was a sunny, positive person and the two of us always got along very well. I was surprised she hadn't called and actually a bit bothered—concluding she didn't care. Here are three ways I could have handled the situation:

**Aggressive:** If I chose to be aggressive, I could have called Julie and left an angry message on her recorder, expressing my disbelief and disappointment in her assumed lack of support. I would respect my wants and needs while giving no consideration to hers.

> **Possible Outcome:** Julie might feel threatened and she would not be inclined to return my call.

**Passive:** If I chose to be passive, I could have kept waiting for Julie to call me, as if leukemia had directly paralyzed my ability to dial out. I would respect her wants and needs (which I could only assume) while ignoring my own.

> **Possible Outcome:** Julie might not call and I would go on being disappointed and feeling sorry for myself.

**Assertive:** If I chose to be assertive, I could have called Julie and left a message, kindly letting her know that I would love to hear from her. I would respect both of our wants and needs, knowing that I would like to talk with her and that I don't have all the information regarding why she hasn't called. She could have been busy, scared or even dealing with her own problems.

> **Possible Outcome:** Julie might call me!

**Actual Communication Used:** After being passive and seeing no results, I chose to be assertive and called Julie. I remembered that I was not the only one who felt fear as I danced with the diagnosis. Others also felt it and sometimes they didn't know what to do or say when it came to my situation. The actual message I left her went something like this:

> "Hey Julie, it's Michelle! I haven't heard from you for a while and, as hard as I try, I can't convince myself that you don't

care! I'd like you to know that I'm okay. In fact, I would love to hear from you! Please call me soon!"

**Actual Outcome:** Guess what happened next? Julie called me back as soon as she got my message! As I had supposed, she had been afraid to call because she didn't know what to say. All she needed was a little encouragement. (**Remember:** Support people need support, too!) In the end, I was happy and so was Julie.

Choosing assertive communication does not always guarantee picture-perfect results, but it does increase the likelihood of establishing communication in which both parties involved feel satisfied with the interaction or at least have an increased understanding of the situation. Assertiveness is not always easy and it requires confrontation. In order to communicate assertively, we need to bring the issues to the table, so to speak. (It is also important to note that aggressive and passive communication styles are not always inappropriate and have their place in some instances.) Simply summarized, there are four basic steps to communicating assertively.

1. **Own your feelings by using I-statements instead of You-statements.**

   I-statements are best used when you have had a strong emotional response to something someone has said or done, and you feel the need to discuss the situation with him or her. Notice the differences in the following sentences:

**Example A: "You are incompetent."**

**Example B: "I am uneasy about the decisions you made concerning my treatment."**

You may very well feel that so-and-so is incompetent, but saying so (Example A) immediately puts him or her on the defensive and sets up an arena of tension. Example B shows ownership of your feelings ("I am uneasy . . .") and keeps the focus on *your perception* of a *specific* situation.

I- statements are made following this model:

I ________________________________ *(feel/think/am/get/etc.)*

when ________________________________ *(neutral description)*

because I ________________________________ *(reason)*

and in the future, ________________________ *(offer next steps).*

For example:

I *feel very frustrated*

when *decisions such as this are made without including me*

because I *need to have an active voice in these treatments*

and in the future, *please include me and hear what I have to say.*

Communication models like the one above are wonderful because they give us a template to follow, but keep in mind that you never want to become formulaic in your responses. Once you get the gist of I-statements, you can adapt the model to your own needs, including some parts of it and excluding others.

2. **Attack the problem, not the person.**

Note how Example B in Item #1 places the specific issue (faulty decision making)—not the person—at the core of the discussion. The statement is direct and specific. The receiver of the message may still get defensive but can now focus on defending the decision making involved, instead of reacting to a personal attack. As shown in the I-statement model, the description of the problem is best stated neutrally, devoid of any interpretation or judgment calls.

This can be a bit trickier to do than it looks. When coaching people on the difference between neutral description and interpretation, I say that we must state only the indisputable facts. We state what we observe, not the interpretation of that event.

For example, suppose you notice a large pile of paperwork on your co-worker's desk. To stay neutral and spotlight the problem, you might say, "I notice all that paperwork on your desk. Do you need some help?" The pile of paperwork is indisputable. It's there and we can see it. An interpretative attack on the person might go something like this: "You're really behind! Do you need some help?" Whether well intentioned or not, the latter statement may put someone on the defensive quite quickly. Even though our assumption may be correct, concluding that a pile of paperwork means that someone is behind on his or her work is interpretative, not neutral. Also, the person—not the paperwork—becomes the inappropriate focus. Attack the problem, not the person.

3. **Avoid conversation fillers and qualifiers.**

   Notice how an assertive message quickly turns passive by the use of fillers and qualifiers:

   **I know you may not like this and please don't take it the wrong way, but I am a little uneasy about the decisions you made . . .**

   Phrases like "I know you might not like this," "don't take it the wrong way" and even "a little" might be intended as politeness, but they place the receiver of such comments in that "one-up," seesaw position, leaving the speaker at a disadvantage. You might as well wrap up all of your power in a pretty box and put a bow on it because you are giving it all away when you use such language. Being assertive does not necessitate being rude, but it does require being direct and affirming one's position.

4. **Match your body language and vocal qualities (nonverbal cues) with your verbal message.**

Imagine that you created the perfect assertive message but delivered it with poor eye contact, a soft voice and lots of ums and uhs. That would knock it back down to a passive level. Those same assertive words might be seen as aggressive if you spoke them sarcastically while your eyebrows were furrowed and your fists were clenched. As you can see, it is essential to congruently match your nonverbal signals with the words you mean.

Nonverbal signals include everything but the actual words you speak. Assertive nonverbal language includes good posture, few weight shifts and casual, appropriate hand gestures. Facial expressions are relaxed, eye contact is direct and a genuine smile or a serious face marks the mood. The vocal qualities that accompany assertive behavior include a smooth rate of speaking (not too fast, not too slow), an even flow and a confident, pleasant tone. Ums and uhs are avoided and laughter is used to accompany only intended humor—not sarcasm or nervousness. Awareness of how your nonverbal signals complement or contradict your words is key.

Control over your own nonverbal cues will obviously be easiest when you are physically feeling well. When you are not, though, you can still try to use appropriately assertive language to get your ideas across or, better yet, coach a caregiver on what to say and how to say it for you.

When you learn to communicate assertively, you earn a ticket that enables you to express yourself effectively. Like sharpening any skill, sending assertive messages does take some initial practice. The next 29 times you say something, you may fall into your old communication patterns, but on that 30th time, you'll stop and realize that communication is about choices and you'll choose to engage in it differently. Even when the results of assertive communication are not as you desire (some people may still respond aggressively or passively, unaware of the choices they have), you'll have the satisfaction of knowing that you expressed your position fairly and responsibly.

When situations arise, try assertive communication with your health care team and with your caregivers. Particularly now, you have a right to express your wants, needs, concerns and fears in a reasonable manner. Repression of any of these leads to pent-up frustration—and that's the last thing you need. As you face your challenges, it is much more comforting to know that you said what needed to be said effectively instead of keeping quiet or getting out of control.[3]

### *Assessing Your Assertiveness Skills*

Carefully read the following scenarios and provide assertive responses for each. Focus on what you would say, how you would say it and what your accompanying nonverbal language (everything but the words) would look like. Possible answers are listed at the end of the exercise.

3. As you practice assertive communication, prepare yourself for the possibility of resistance from others. Your new communication patterns may be met with surprise. If this becomes the case, discuss your communication choices with others. In essence, *talk about your talk.* Let others know that you are attempting to express your wants and needs as responsibly and effectively as possible.

**Example:** Due to her chemotherapy treatments, Emily has recently lost all of her long hair. She's handling the change well but is still nervous about her new look. She chooses to cover up with hats and turbans. One night, a distant friend stops by unannounced to check in on Emily. As they sit and chat, the smiling friend aggressively tells Emily to take off her hat because she really wants to see her scalp. Though the visitor means well, Emily is caught off guard and immediately feels uncomfortable. She doesn't want to take off her hat and she doesn't want to be rude to her guest. What should she say?

**Possible Response:** "No, I am not comfortable with that right now."

> Emily claims her own feelings and does not need to offer any explanation that might lead to more discussion on the topic.

**Alternate Response:** She could thank the friend for her acceptance and encouragement while politely refusing the offer.

**Nonverbal Cues:** Direct eye contact, steady voice, slight smile.

**Note:** Placing boundaries around your comfort zones is acceptable and necessary. Hair loss for a man or woman is an extremely personal thing. Make sure that you protect yourself as needed throughout this process. In the above situation, Emily could sternly repeat her message (this time without the smile) if her intrusive friend persisted (this is known as "escalating assertion"). Also notice that no apologies are necessary.

***Now you try . . .***

1. Because he was already in remission, Alex's treatments were more preventative at this point and considered to be nonemergency procedures. One cold day, he waited in the clinic for his next dose of chemotherapy. The first nurse he encountered tried to inject the I.V. needle into his arm, but she missed the vein; a second nurse tried twice with no luck. Finally, a pediatric nurse pointed to a strong vein, but that didn't work either. By this fourth attempt, Alex was truly feeling like a pin cushion. What could he say?

   **Possible Assertive Response:**

   **Nonverbal Cues:**

2. Carmen was sitting in the hospital, thankful to be getting the blood transfusion her body needed. Everything was going smoothly and Carmen was feeling optimistic and cheerful. To help pass the time, she decided to call her sister, Rachel. Rachel was happy to hear from Carmen, but when she heard that her little sister was in the middle of a blood transfusion, she exclaimed, "Gross! I don't know how you can go through all of this! I know I couldn't!" Carmen's mood began to plummet. She had never thought of the transfusion that way. What could she say to Rachel?

**Possible Assertive Response:**

**Nonverbal Cues:**

### *Possible Assertive Answers*

1. **Response:** "I have had enough. We've tried this four times with no luck and I've decided that I'd like to go home and come back tomorrow. May I please speak with my doctor?"

   Alex starts off by using an I-statement, then neutrally describes the problem (instead of attacking the nurses' failed attempts). He also empowers himself by asking to speak with someone else.

   **Nonverbal Cues:** Serious tone; direct eye contact; strong, steady voice; no smile.

   **Note:** Know your rights as a patient. Typically, if a health care professional is unable to effectively insert a needle in two tries, then you may request someone else. Trust your body. *If your treatment is not an emergency procedure* and things aren't going well, ask your doctor or case manager what other options you have. Emotional well-being is as important as physical well-being. Deal from your strengths (knowing your body, effective communication), not your weaknesses (fear, frustration).

2. **Response:** "I know you find this upsetting, but I feel discouraged when you react to my medical procedures so negatively. The best thing you can do for me right now is to keep things positive!"

    Carmen appears empathetic to her sister's feelings, yet she still maintains respect for her own needs. She attacks the problem (the reaction) instead of her sister and claims her own feelings with an I-statement.

    **Nonverbal Cues:** Voice is understanding and upbeat, yet serious and without hesitation or qualifiers.

    **Alternate Response:** Carmen may have chosen to get off the phone right away. Later, when she was in a better position, she could have assertively approached her sister. She also could have asked a caregiver or patient advocate to talk to her sister for her.

## KEY CONCEPTS: COMMUNICATE ASSERTIVELY

- Particularly now, you have wants, concerns and fears that need to be expressed.
- Assertive communication is the direct, honest way of expressing ideas while respecting yourself and others.
- Communicating assertively is synonymous with communicating responsibly.
- Sending assertive messages requires:
  1. Using I-statements.
  2. Attacking the problem, not the person.
  3. Avoiding conversation fillers and qualifiers.
  4. Matching your nonverbal cues (tone, rate and vocal volume along with all body language such as posture and facial expressions) with your spoken words.
- Communicate from strength, not weakness.

## PUT IT TO PRACTICE

Would you consider yourself to be aggressive, passive or assertive? What would someone close to you think? Many of us glide through all three communication patterns depending on the people and situations involved. The first part of changing your communication is determining how it might help you. Then figure out with whom and when it might be most appropriate. Anticipate their reaction so you can prepare to hold your ground.

***Make a plan to be more assertive today.***

1. I will be more assertive with:

2. Specifically, I will say:

3. I think he/she/they might react this way:

4. I will reward my new behavior by: *(do something that makes you happy! Get ice cream, buy yourself a plant, etc.)*

## *Thoughts and Notes*

*"The proper task of communication is to create love and harmony among us. It is peacemaking."*
*—M. Scott Peck*

# Empower Yourself

Surround yourself

with empowering words,

thoughts, perspectives

and people.

LESSON

# 4

# Take Control of Your Health Care

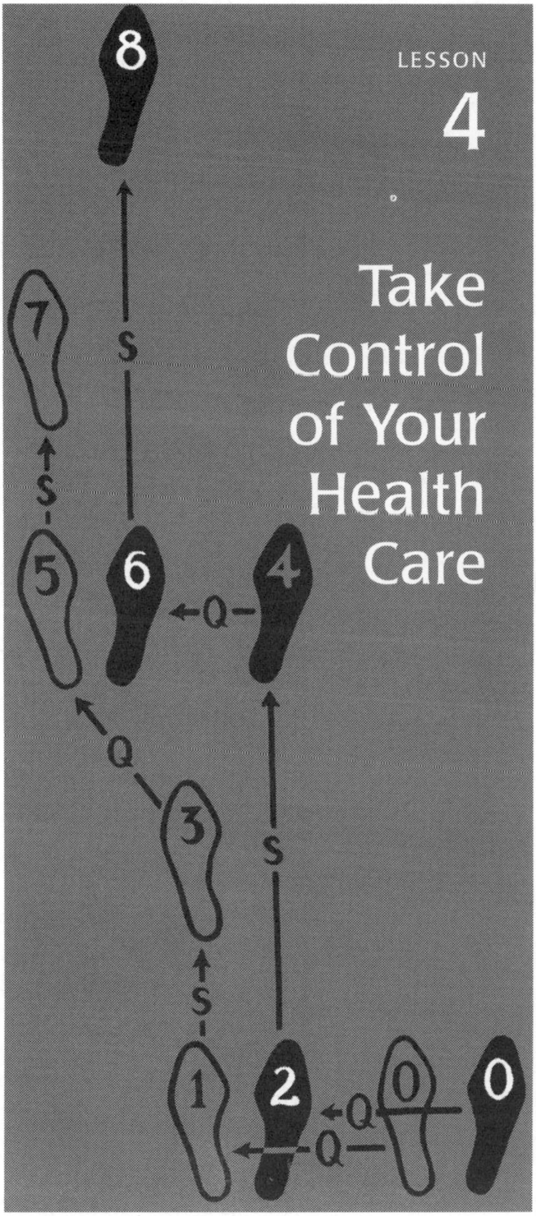

For me, leukemia was like a password that opened the doors to a medical world about which I had many misconceptions. As I stepped into this new land, I knew exactly what role I expected my doctors to play. I wanted them to be brilliant, empathetic individuals who had nothing else to do but tend to my physical and emotional needs. They were to be warm, patient and always attentive. Unfortunately, but not surprisingly, the doctors never read from the script I had prepared. Brilliant they were, but they didn't always have the time or training to be the compassionate beings I sought. That's when I realized I had the power to change my perspective.

If I could not have it all from my physicians, then I would just give them a smaller part in this performance. I decided that they would be solely responsible for my physical well-being. They would diagnose my case, investigate my symptoms and prescribe the best treatment plans. Instead of seeing them as actors in my play, I began to see them as employees whom I had carefully selected for the specific task at hand.

Because it was difficult for me to fully comprehend my diagnosis on a scientific level, I was satisfied leaving the Physical Me to the physicians. To achieve balance, however, I dubbed myself Chief Executive Officer of the Emotional and Spiritual Me. I investigated complementary forms of healing—from meditation to homeopathy. I steadfastly practiced positive thinking and prayer, and I sought stable shoulders big enough for me to lean on when necessary. My new "promotion," spurred by a change in perspective, granted me a portion of the control and participation that I desperately needed.

This separation of roles—physical and emotional—worked extremely well at times. For example, in the early stage of my treatment, my doctors prescribed a new "wonder drug" that was meant to accelerate the growth of my immature white blood cells. Prescribing the medicine was consistent with their position as my physicians: They were to take care of the Physical Me. My job as C.E.O. of the Emotional and Spiritual Me was to *believe* in the treatment. I did so by saying some sort of prayer or affirmation *every single time* I took the pills (that meant twice a day for 28 days).

Sometimes I would give thanks for the knowledge my doctors had, for the advancements in medicine and for the opportunity to live in a time and place where I could receive such treatments. Other days, I would pray that my body would accept and respond well to the medication. Still other times, I would simply hold the pills in my hands and say, "Okay, do your stuff!" I believed in the chemotherapy treatments I chose, deciding that C.H.E.M.O. stood for **C**hrist **H**ealing **E**verything **M**ichelle **O**wns. My belief in my physician's plan and my active participation in my healing process were powerful recovery tools.

From my perspective, the medical team had their job and I had mine. I assumed our tasks were mutually exclusive, but sometimes I admittedly longed for a softer, more human approach from my physicians. For instance, one morning shortly after the diagnosis, I received a disturbing message on my answering machine. One of my doctors dryly said, "Michelle needs to receive chemotherapy today. Come to the hospital as soon as possible." I was dumbfounded. I had never before received chemotherapy and my first dose wasn't scheduled for another two weeks. "Why today? What's the hurry?" I frantically asked my husband, "Will it hurt? Will I get sick?"

Because I lived an hour away from the hospital, I also had concerns about my lodging. Would I need to stay close to the hospital just in case my body didn't respond well to the treatment? Should I pack? WHO WILL TAKE CARE OF MY DOG? I had so many questions. Reality was beginning to set in and I was psychologically unprepared for this experience. I was angered by the nonchalance of that answering-machine message. I called back to get some answers and received the same sterile disposition. Apparently for some physicians, giving chemotherapy orders is as routine as taking a patient's temperature. No wonder this doctor had become numb.

The next day, when I was face to face with my medical team, I expressed my concerns and frustrations with the chemotherapy ordeal. I asked that they see me as **more than blood and bone marrow**. I then knew that our roles *must* overlap. I could not remain completely oblivious to the clinical part of my health issues and the doctors could not treat me as "just another cancer patient." After ironing out the initial wrinkles, the communication between my medical team and me was primarily effective. We maintained a reciprocal relationship of listening, questioning and respecting each other's position.

Incredible as they may be, health care professionals are human, too. Sometimes they get tired; they are often overworked and are not exempt from making mistakes. With this reminder that they are human comes permission to communicate with them.

We have permission to say:

- Please recheck my temperature. I don't think that reading was accurate.
- I don't understand. Will you please clarify that for me?
- I've received a lot of conflicting information lately. What is correct?
- Is this side effect normal?
- I am at my saturation point. Do I have any choices about the rest of my treatments?
- Do we have to do this now? Can we wait an hour, a week or do nothing?
- I am uncomfortable with this nurse. Please have someone else tend to me.
- I am more than this diagnosis. Please see me as such.
- No more.

We also have permission to say:

- Thank you!
- Good job!
- I appreciate all you have done.

**Remember:** You know yourself better than any physician ever could. You know when you are confused and when you need more information. You know when your body aches and when it doesn't. *Do not be afraid to communicate with your doctors!* It would make more sense to be afraid if you *didn't* communicate with them.

***And when you aren't able to communicate with your doctors . . .***

Because of my background in communication studies, I am typically comfortable dealing with most people. Still, throughout my dance with the diagnosis, there were times when I was too fatigued or sedated to communicate with anyone, particularly my doctors; other times, I was just plain intimidated. For these reasons, I highly recommend that every patient have an effective patient advocate at her or his side. This person might be affiliated with the hospital or, more likely, might be a friend or relative who can assertively speak for you when you can't.

**Effective patient advocates:**

- consistently have the patient's best interest in mind
- are comfortable speaking with people at all levels and at all times
- are familiar with general medical procedures and policies
- stay positive for the patient
- put the patient's interests above their own

- are good listeners
- are able to remain objective in emotional situations
- share a mutual trust with the patient
- practice appropriate assertiveness

Aside from being great caregivers, my husband, my mom and my aunt all served as terrific patient advocates. I was also assigned a phenomenal case manager. She was present during most of my office visits and served as an official liaison between my doctors and me. She often provided the empathy that the other members of my health care team lacked and, whenever possible, I ran most of my medical questions and concerns by her before taking them further. Whether someone is assigned through the hospital or is a confident caregiver, having an effective patient advocate is a must in today's health care world.

## KEY CONCEPTS: TAKE CONTROL OF YOUR HEALTH CARE

- Choose to take an active part in your healing process.
- Trust that you know yourself better than any physician ever could.
- Health care professionals are human (just like you) and you have the right to communicate with them.
- Set up two-way communication with your doctors.

- When possible, designate an effective patient advocate who takes over when you have difficulties communicating with your doctors.

## PUT IT TO PRACTICE

Promote yourself to C.E.O. of the Emotional and Spiritual Y-O-U! After accepting this highly acclaimed position, write out answers to the following questions:

1. With this title, what specifically are your job responsibilities?

2. What does a day in the life of the C.E.O. of the Emotional and Spiritual Y-O-U look like? For example, how do you start your morning? End your day?

3. Are you capable of the task?

4. Do you need to appoint an assistant (someone who will help keep you at your best)? If so, who will that be?

## *Thoughts and Notes*

*"It isn't until you come to a spiritual understanding of who you are—not necessarily a religious feeling, but deep down, the spirit within, that you can begin to take control."*
*—Oprah Winfrey*

## GET OUTSIDE OF YOURSELF

*Cancer can be all-consuming.*

*When you're up to it, send a little love someone else's way.*

■ **Write a letter complimenting a caring doctor.**

Commend his or her interpersonal skills or intellect. Be specific and give examples. Send the original to the chief of staff or head of the department and send a copy to the outstanding physician.

■ **Acknowledge others who might be in need.**

Does your Aunt Karen have a cold? Sure, a cold may not seem like much in comparison to chemotherapy, but we all know that colds feel crummy! Let her know that you wish her well. Support your support people!

■ **Write a letter of praise about an extra-special nurse.**

What makes this nurse so special? Is he funny in stressful situations? Is she a great listener? Is she calm under pressure? Write a note highlighting the details and send it to the nursing supervisor. Acknowledge the nurse with a box of chocolates "wrapped" with your letter.

■ **Encourage others to talk about their lives.**

Sometimes people are afraid to talk about themselves because, compared to what you're going through, they see their everyday events as trivial. Let them know you want to hear about their lives! Remind them that it's often nice to talk about anything *but* disease.

■ **Donate a toy to a children's hospital.**

Take a special toy or stuffed animal to the registration desk at a children's hospital or wing. Ask that it be delivered to a girl or boy in need of a smile.

■ **Send thank-you notes to people who have made you smile.**

Keep stationery with you when you are in the clinic or hospital. Write letters of appreciation to your caregivers, your special neighbor, the nurse's aide . . . anyone who has brightened your day along this journey.

**HELPING OTHERS HELPS YOU!**

LESSON

# 5

# Learn to F.L.Y. (Fully Love Yourself)

Disease often has a strange way of turning us against our bodies at times when we need to be embracing them. Sometimes we feel betrayed by our bodies and shudder at the changes in our appearance (most notably the hair loss and scars). For me, however, disease had the opposite affect: I learned to love my body instead of loathe it.

For much of my early adult life, I struggled with the eating disorder bulimia. Even years after I stopped the physical binge-purge cycle, I still continued the mental abuse associated with the dysfunction. "I hate my body," "I'm fat" and "I'm ugly" were my daily mantras. Obsession over my appearance, along with feelings of worthlessness, kept me from enjoying some of the simplest pleasures in life—from fun times with my friends to intimate moments with my husband. When I was diagnosed with leukemia, all of that changed. Suddenly, I was labeled with a life-threatening disease and *no one could tell me how I got it.* I carefully considered what role my abusive thoughts could have played.

Supporting my gut feeling, Alan Cohen, author of *The Dragon Doesn't Live Here Anymore,* explains that the body is the last place dysfunction shows itself. He claims that it starts first in the mind, moves to the emotions and finally, if we have still ignored all the red flags, it appears in the body. His explanation doesn't work for me when I think of all of the innocent children who fight disease, but it did cause me to ponder my own adult illness. Even the *chance* that this information might be true—that my thoughts could have encouraged the cancer that was present in my bloodstream—caused me to rethink my ways.

When I was diagnosed with leukemia, I didn't feel like my body had betrayed me. I felt like I had betrayed my body. Two days after my initial diagnosis, the blurry image in my mind came into complete focus: *I could no longer afford to berate my body.* I saw no other option but to embrace it "as is." So I did.

With cancer, God handed me a desperately needed pair of corrective lenses. Physically, the thighs I thought were unsightly I now appreciated for their strength. I accepted the too-wide waist. On an internal level, the leukemic cells that would not mature were not hated but I, instead, saw them as a system malfunction that needed to be lovingly corrected. In many ways, leukemia cured me of bulimia.

One of my most peaceful moments came between chemotherapy treatments on a day when I was alone at the beach. Stretching out in the sand, I mindfully focused on every part of my body—from ticklish toes to hairless head—and I completed the following phrase accordingly:

**I am thankful for my** ______________________ *(body part)*

**because** ______________________________ *(reason)*.

For example, I shouted, "I am thankful for my toes because they can feel the sand!" or "I am thankful for my arms because they open wide and receive lots of love and hugs!" I gained a feeling of oneness with my body and soul by practicing this simple exercise. I also had many reasons to smile.

Please let me remind you that this self-love and gentleness was new to me. I had tried it countless times before but it never seemed genuine. Now my self-acceptance was not only obligatory . . . *it was real.* With this new love, I could see that the healing taking place inside me was not only at a cellular level: *it encompassed my entire being.* I believe this disposition did wonders for my recovery. Simply said, it is much easier to focus on the more important parts of life and living when you are not preoccupied with separation from your self.

If there is only one lesson that you take from this book, make it this one: **Learn to F.L.Y.** (or **F**ully **L**ove **Y**ourself). Fully love your being: who you are now and how you have taken form. This self-love I advocate has nothing to do with the ego or narcissism, but much to do with accepting your God-given birthright to be at peace with yourself, inside and out. Fully loving yourself is not about ignoring the anger, doubt or fears you may have. It is about being gentle with yourself through the acknowledgement of these emotions.

It is attained by working through negative self-talk and accepting yourself (both body and soul) "as is." Any personal changes you choose to make when fully loving yourself come from a place of clarity and kindness rather than judgment and dislike. Think of it this way: an effective, successful C.E.O. (of the Emotional and Spiritual Y-O-U) would have it no other way.

Learning to F.L.Y. is an ongoing process. Several ways to help you earn your pilot's license include the following:

1. **Keep a journal.** Buy yourself a beautiful blank book and some colorful pens. Jot down the positive and negative parts of your journey. A journal is not only a terrific way to record your ex-

periences for future reference, but it also serves as a sounding board of sorts. It is a safe place to explore fears and tensions. Like a good friend, a journal "listens" without judgment and helps you sort out your experiences. It also helps you clarify your goals and focus on forward movement.

If you are not used to journaling, commit to the process—it may take some time for you to become comfortable with it. It is very worth the effort! Take your journal everywhere. At the end of each entry, try to list things for which you are thankful. Look at what you have instead of what you do not have. Count your blessings. Write letters to God. You may also get started by recording the activities from this book in your journal. Get ready to start writing and start learning more about your wonderful self.

2. **Strengthen your spiritual muscle.** Pray, seek a higher power and affirm your values and beliefs. Pray BIG prayers, not little ones! Pray for your healing: physical, mental and spiritual. Define your higher purpose; align yourself with it, then live it.

3. **Talk back to negative self-talk.** Whether attacking the body or the soul, negative self-talk says, "I'm not good enough as I am." Oddly enough, this type of talk serves a protective purpose. Sometimes it masks feelings of fear or insecurity. The idea behind it is often, "Nothing and no one can hurt me if I hurt myself first." Identify negative self-talk when you hear it

*and then be gentle with yourself.* Berating yourself for berating yourself will get you nowhere! Ask yourself questions such as, "Why am I thinking these thoughts?" and "What triggered this response?" *Trace your feelings back to their roots and nurture them.* The next time a similar thought comes along, say to it, "I know why you are here and there is no need for you anymore. *I am taking care of myself at all levels!* "

After acknowledging that the negative self-talk is no longer necessary, choose a more constructive way of looking at your situation. Effectively ridding your mind of clutter requires recognition of the behavior followed by self-exploration and, finally, the decision to see things differently. Use your sense of humor, too! Whenever a friend of mine notices herself going down the path of self-bashing, she pauses and says rather dryly, "Oh yes, and then there's *that* thought." She acknowledges it and then chooses thoughts that take her where she wants to be.

4. **Build up your support team.** Surround yourself with positive individuals. If someone in your immediate support team is particularly negative, lovingly let her or him know that negativity has no place in your plan to heal. It's much easier to stay positive when in the company of other positive beings and, let's face it, now more than ever you need to be cognizant of the energy within and around you.

5. **Believe in yourself.** Anatole France said, "To accomplish great things we must not only act, but also dream, not only plan, but also believe." Believe you are worth it! Believe you can F.L.Y!

6. **Be patient with yourself.** As with most things that are worthwhile, learning to F.L.Y. takes time and practice. Still, it is one of, if not *the,* most important things you will do in your healing process. At times, I still struggle with self-love. Despite all my dedication to the process, sometimes an old tape will resurface, cruelly shouting that I am inadequate.

   When I am in a space of fully loving myself ("as is," flaws and all), I can turn off the tape and remind myself that those tunes are not what my life is all about anymore. I make a conscious decision to move on to more empowering thoughts. I've moved on to a CD player and those old tapes just don't work anymore! But when that tape is playing too loudly for me to talk over, I realize I am in the need of some refresher "flying" lessons and I start over with Step #1. Please be patient with yourself. Learning to F.L.Y. is an ongoing process.

7. **Seek professional counseling when needed.** Believing you can achieve self-acceptance does not always mean that you can or should do it alone. Sometimes a counselor or psychologist, specifically one trained in the areas of esteem and disease, is the best option. Ask your physician for referrals.

If you are still not convinced that you need to F.L.Y. through disease, remember the old saying that life is not a dress rehearsal. Diagnosis or not, *this is it.* Spending time dwelling on the negative is so wasteful! It is the positive that enriches the experience of living. When I think of all the countless times I wouldn't fully participate in life because I shied away from the inner beauty of my being, I am deeply saddened. But when I think that disease, of all things, gave me the wake-up call I needed to truly accept myself, and with that, gave me the chance to live every day I have left to its fullest, I am grateful for the second chance. Knowing what I know now, I would gladly trade a lifetime of separation from my self for an undetermined amount of time spent while fully loving who I am. All said, learning to F.L.Y. does not come without hard work and dedication to the task.

**Remember:** you are worth the effort! I am giving each of you a pilot's license . . . now go F.L.Y!

***Highly Recommended Readings for Those Learning to F.L.Y.***

The practice of self-acceptance is a complex subject that deserves thorough exploration. In this chapter, I offered only a taste of its importance. The reference list below contains several time-tested books that helped me develop a better sense of self. Each teaches self-acceptance in wonderful yet varied ways. These insightful authors have so much to show us. Pick up any of these books and get ready for class to begin!

- *Living, Loving and Learning* by Leo Buscaglia, Ph.D.
- *Taming Your Gremlin* by Richard D. Carson
- *The Dragon Doesn't Live Here Anymore* by Alan Cohen, Ph.D.
- *You Can Heal Your Life* by Louise Hay
- *Love is Letting Go of Fear* by Gerald G. Jampolsky, Ph.D.
- *The Power of Positive Thinking* by Norman Vincent Peale
- *Succulent Wild Woman* by SARK
- *Tough Times Never Last, But Tough People Do!* by Dr. Robert H. Schuller
- *A Return to Love* by Marianne Williamson

## KEY CONCEPTS: LEARN TO F.L.Y. (FULLY LOVE YOURSELF)

- One of the most important things you can do for yourself is to learn to F.L.Y. (Fully Love Yourself).
- Now more than ever, you need to accept and embrace your body, not turn against it.
- Fully loving yourself requires being gentle with yourself as you travel through all of your emotions.
- It is much easier to focus on the more important parts of healing when you are not preoccupied with separation from your self.
- Learning to F.L.Y. is an ongoing process. Seek outside support and in-depth sources of information to help you along the way.

## PUT IT TO PRACTICE

Try the exercise I practiced at the beach. It will only take a minute; you can do it anywhere and the results are uplifting.

1. Choose three of your physical attributes and complete this sentence:

   **I am thankful for my** ______________________________ *(body part)*

   **because** ____________________________________________ *(reason)*.

   Don't spend too much time searching for the "right" attribute or the "right" reason. Say the first thing that comes to your mind, censoring only if it is negative. Laughing is allowed!

2. Choose three qualities of your personality (for example, your sharp wit, generosity or eye for detail) and complete the sentence again:

   **I am thankful for my** ______________________________ *(quality)*

   **because** ____________________________________________ *(reason)*.

   Don't feel obligated to stop at three. Journal the results. You are AMAZING!

## *Thoughts and Notes*

*"My goal is to love myself more than I did yesterday."*
*—Louise Hay*

# Love Yourself

Learn to F.L.Y.

Fully Love Yourself

LESSON

# 6

# Learn to F.L.Y. While Losing Your Hair

Many of us who choose to heal our bodies through chemotherapy are bound to lose our hair. I was told I would lose my hair within three to four weeks after receiving the type of chemotherapy required for my treatment. This scared me for a couple of reasons. First, as a woman in an image-obsessed society, I didn't know how I'd handle it. Would I still feel feminine? Would I be able to look in the mirror and truly accept who looked back at me? Would my husband still find me attractive? Sure, I was practicing the art of fully loving myself "as is," but I was forging into new territory.

The second thing that bothered me was that losing my hair would put me in the visual cancer group. Until I lost my hair, I still had days in which to appear "cancerless" to those who didn't know better. A bald head would signify my official initiation into the cancer club.

One night, I contemplated the power of mind over matter and its relation to hair loss. Maybe I could *will* my hair to stay in. After all, I heard that some people never lost their hair despite receiving chemotherapy. Maybe I could be one of those! As if answering a question I hadn't yet asked, the next thought in my mind was "Rebirth." I understood immediately. As a child is born with little hair, my hair loss would mark my personal rebirth into a new life of fully loving myself . . . as is. Acceptance replaced vanity.

***Hair loss is a very small price to pay for an extension of your life.***

Each of our experiences may differ; for me, the physical process of losing my hair was much more upsetting than actually being bald. Before my first round of chemo, I had my shoulder-length locks cut short. I thought it would be easier to deal with short hair when it fell out, but it wasn't. The truth was that, no matter what the length, I couldn't stand having strands of hair falling out all over my clothes, in the bathtub and on my pillow. I felt like Charlie Brown's Christmas tree: One touch and pieces of my hair fell out like dried pine needles!

My husband, Brian, had the perfect remedy. "Let's shave it!" he enthusiastically offered. Seeing an opportunity for some control, I agreed. If losing my hair was not optional, I'd be in charge of how, where and when.

Brian got the clippers and we went outside. As he shaved away, I let him know that this was the one and only time he'd ever cut my hair! He made it magical, though. He repeatedly told me he loved me and said that I was beautiful—hair or no hair. We laughed with nervous excitement as he said, "*This* is for all the times we've been late because of your hair!" He asked me to sing Sinead O'Connor songs and I did. What could have been an extremely emotional time *was* . . . but the emotions present were love and laughter, not the fear and sadness I had anticipated.

Eleven days passed before I looked at my bald scalp in the mirror. I decided that I would see it when I was ready to see it. When I finally took a peek, I wasn't *thrilled* with what I saw, but I didn't despise it either. I accepted it for what it was. I then realized that my beauty, my femininity, my being was not in my hair—it was in my soul.

As I became used to my new look, I marveled at my scalp. It was so smooth, so delicate. It needed special care: sunscreen or hats on sunny days (trust me, a burnt scalp is not fun) and cotton nightcaps to keep it warm at night. My scalp also needed to be loved, not scorned. Someone once told me to experience rain on my naked head. When I got the chance, I did. It was wonderful!

My hair was approximately one inch long when my treatments ended and I was temporarily free from clinic visits. Proud of my success and more comfortable with my thinly covered scalp, I didn't want to wear my wigs anymore. My newly sprouting hair was testament to my accomplishments. Sometimes, though, I felt a bit awkward in public. I (or Brian) had to remind me that fully loving myself still meant "as is," with or without hair or wigs.

A few times, male acquaintances whom I hadn't seen for a while would actually stop me and say with disbelief, "What happened to your hair?" Mentally prepared for such comments, I would muster all the enthusiasm I could and reply, "Isn't it great? I'm recovering from cancer!" The look on their faces was well worth the self-disclosure. Losing my hair and growing it back made me a braver and more confident person. It can do the same for you.

Again and again, my experiences taught me that we have many options to see things differently. You, too, can choose to F.L.Y. through all situations. As you soar, watch for the amazing changes that follow!

### *A Word About Wigs . . .*

Two weeks before my husband shaved my head, I went wig shopping with my mom. Everyone we talked to said to shop for a wig *before* losing my hair. They were right and I advise you to do the same if you choose to get a wig. It is easier to match up your color and style this way, and you may be more comfortable going from shop to shop while your hair is still there and you are feeling well.

I was nervous as we entered the first wig salon. It was another "How did I get here?" moment. To my relief, the salespeople were great and my mom and I actually had fun! I soon looked at the "problem" of getting a wig as an opportunity. I could change colors, styles and lengths instantly! The first wig I chose was close to my natural color, though longer and thicker. Later, I bought a shorter, dark wig at a shop where the woman called me "sweet pea." I even got a "chemotherapy discount" at one salon. Who knew? My mom also bought me several stylish turbans and caps to wear with or without the wigs.

So why buy wigs if I was really accepting myself "as is"? Well, the wigs provided me with the option of looking inconspicuous when I just wanted to be "Michelle," not "Michelle, the-woman-who-is-obviously-going-through-chemotherapy." They also helped me feel a bit more feminine at times when I needed extra validation.

If choosing a wig seems like the right thing for you, then I have some suggestions. Aside from shopping for your wig early, I advise you to take someone along whose opinion you trust. Shop with someone who can help you with the decision-making process. Don't let yourself be talked into something that isn't you. Make sure your choice is one you really like and will really wear.

**Remember:** You are seeking comfort for potentially uncomfortable times. Go to several wig shops. (Most hospitals have referral lists.)

Some shops will be better than others. One shop I visited was proof of that. The owner worked out of her modest home and kept all of her wigs outside in a shed! Aside from the fact that her styles were extremely outdated and a bit musty, she actually tried to talk me into a red wig by telling me that I didn't look good as a blond—even though that was my natural color. Luckily, the experience provided my mom and me with belly-aching laughter for days!

## KEY CONCEPTS: LEARN TO F.L.Y. WHILE LOSING YOUR HAIR

- Hair loss gives you another great opportunity to F.L.Y!
- You have many options to see things differently.
- Hair loss is a very small price to pay for an extension of your life.
- You may choose to shave your head through the hair-loss process. This gives you an opportunity for control.
- If you have never done so, experience rain on your naked scalp. What a thrill!

***If you choose to cover your head . . .***

- Check your insurance. Many insurance companies cover a certain amount of wig purchases if your doctor writes a prescription for a "cranial prosthesis."
- Get a wig before you lose your hair.
- Take someone with you whose opinion you trust.
- Shop around.
- Don't be talked into something that isn't "you."
- Wear your new hats and turbans around before you lose your hair in order to ease the transition.
- Dare to have some fun!

## PUT IT TO PRACTICE

If losing your hair is a frightening prospect, spend some time processing your feelings about it. What worries you the most about losing your hair? Why? What options do you have for gaining control or seeing this differently? What good could possibly come from losing your hair? Whether it be a caregiver, professional or a current cancer fighter or survivor, who might be the best person to receive support from in this area? Visit Lessons 2 and 7 for information on changing perspective and managing anger.

## *Thoughts and Notes*

*"The fundamental problem that most patients have is an inability to love themselves."*
*—Bernie S. Siegel, M.D.*

LESSON

# 7

# Acknowledge Anger

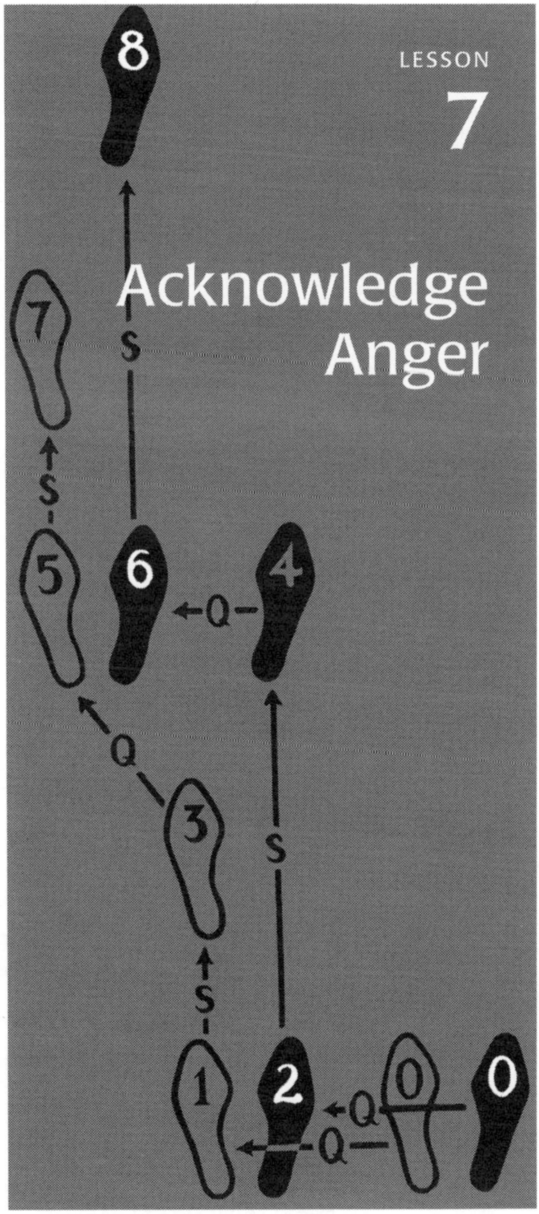

As you may know firsthand by now, the type of anger that stems from the diagnosis of a disease like cancer is an extremely powerful emotion. It should neither be ignored nor invited to move in. Ignoring it is a denial of the self and may ultimately lead to an explosive outburst. Inviting anger in to stay too long might point to a path of negativity that could greatly impede the healing process. The balance lies in a healthy acknowledgement and expression of anger as it arises.

It would be unusual to go through a challenge such as ours and not get angry at some point. Some of us get angry upon news of the initial diagnosis. "Why me?" and "I don't have time for this!" and "This isn't fair!" are typical thoughts that blaze like untamed fire through our minds. Some of us don't get angry until later on when things are not going as we had expected or hoped.

My first major experience with anger fell into the latter category. One night, well into my chemotherapy treatments, I noticed that my eyebrows and eyelashes were falling out. My medical team had assured me that this wouldn't happen with the specific type of chemo I was receiving. I had prepared myself for losing the hair on my head—that I could handle. I had not prepared myself for losing the hair that framed my eyes. Silly as it sounds now, I felt mad, sad, ugly, out of control and downright furious.

The spiritual teachings of *A Course in Miracles* say that you are never upset for the reason you think you are. Remembering this belief prompted me to further investigate my feelings. After digging a bit deeper, I acknowledged that yes, losing all my facial hair scared me, but what was really causing my angry panic was the fact that *no one could accurately tell me what to expect through my treatments.* I kept getting these "rare," unexpected reactions and, while I believed that everything was happening for a reason, the facial hair triggered my breaking point. I didn't think I could handle anymore surprises. I liked my eyebrows and I wanted to keep them. Until this point, I had smiled through all the tough times. Not anymore! That night I broke down. I didn't want anyone to reframe my issues for me. I didn't want to hear how much worse it could be or how lucky I was. I just wanted to be ANGRY!

I didn't stifle my anger because, quite honestly, I couldn't. I cried, I yelled and I pouted. This went on for most of the evening. Only after getting it out was I able to move on and find constructive ways to deal with my anger.

More likely than not, somewhere, sometime you will get mad. The following suggestions make it possible to experience and deal with anger constructively—not at the expense of yourself, your healing or those around you.

1. **Give yourself permission to feel the anger.** Some will argue that anger has no place in your healing. I assert that it does and that the only way to get over it is to acknowledge its presence before moving through it. You can yell, punch a punching bag, empty your mind in a journal or cry it out with someone. Do what works *for you*. You might release anger by doing something you love, like surfing, painting or walking with your dog. Get outside, if possible.

No matter what you do, respect your anger and be present with it . . . this, too, is a part of your dance.

Anger signals us when something isn't right. Maybe you aren't getting the information or the attention that you need; maybe you are scared about your future; maybe you just can't keep that smile on for another minute. No matter what the reason, **it is okay to be angry**. It *is not* okay to stay angry for extended periods of time without resolution, but *it is* okay to initially react in anger to the uncertainties around you. Welcome your anger . . . just don't let it stay too long.

If your anger becomes more of an extended habit than a healthy expression of frustration, **put a time limit on it**. For example, tell yourself that you will allow yourself to be angry until 4:00 PM on Saturday. This works! When 4:00 PM Saturday comes around (if you can actually stay angry until then), commit to advancing through the next steps of resolving angry emotions. Be specific with your time constraints. Perhaps you'll allow yourself only five more minutes; perhaps five days. Allow adequate time for expression of anger while also acknowledging your eventual need to move through it.

When feeling angry (or soon afterward), ask yourself:

- *What emotion* is at the base of my anger? Is it fear, frustration, sadness, guilt, pain or some combination of emotions (e.g., I am feeling very helpless)?

2. **After feeling your anger's presence, you need to deal with it.** Kicking your couch might make you feel better for a moment, but it does nothing to permanently rid you of the roots of that anger. Dealing with it requires a deeper exploration of its purpose and your options. When possible, be specific about your anger. Ask yourself the following questions:

   - *What* am I so angry about (e.g., rare reactions to my treatments)?

   - *Why* is this so upsetting to me (e.g., I feel so out of control; I never know what to expect)?

   - *How* will I effectively deal with this (e.g., I'll shift my perspective when ready; I'll seek out a support group; I'll pray for strength and acceptance)?

I know, I know. Some of you are questioning how the heck you'd know the answers to these questions. Trust me: *You know.* If you're convinced you don't know, then ask yourself "What if I *did* know?" and ask yourself the questions again. It's amazing how intuitive we are when we become still and listen.

Writing in a journal is one of my favorite ways to expose the tangled roots of anger. Writing is a release. My journal provides me with a safe place to explore my fears. The pages never judge me!

Start by answering the questions above, or perhaps you might have a conversation with anger, asking it about its origin, purpose and needs. Again, you know these answers. It's all a matter of mindfulness coupled with a willingness to "go there." If reflecting or writing doesn't work for you, discuss your anger with someone you trust. There's a saying that goes, "When you lose your head, go and borrow someone else's until you find yours!" We need to talk to someone who has it together when we don't. A clear mind is more insightful than a muddled one.

3. **When working with anger, the final step is to heal it.** Healing anger is the action step that follows dealing with it. When you are ready, act on the options you listed for dealing with your anger. For example, make that call to a support group, change your perspective or sit down and say that prayer! If your anger was spurred by problems with health care professionals or one of your caregivers, take the time to talk with them. (Try to approach people *after* you have worked through your anger and you are in a space where you can speak to them assertively, not aggressively.) Exploration of anger without the action step leaves the wound open, ready to irritate again—only worse—in the future. Only after feeling, dealing with and healing your anger, it is time to move on to other parts of your journey.

### *Post Script*

Ironically, my most extreme feelings of anger came *after* I had written this chapter and *after* I had put full closure on my dance with the diagnosis. When all of my chemotherapy treatments were complete, my attending physician said that he was confident that I had progressed as planned, but he still needed one final bone-marrow biopsy to prove it. I viewed this biopsy as the "last hurrah" and I was a good sport about it. To me, this biopsy signified that I had gone full circle. I welcomed its symbolism.

Later in the week, the chromosome test from the biopsy came back negative, just as we hoped. It showed that everything seemed to be back to normal. Hurray! My doctor was pleased and assumed that the results from the cellular test he ordered would follow suit. A new lab that lacked the ability to expedite results performed that test, however, so we didn't know for sure. Weeks went by—still no results. My doctor said not to worry and I didn't. I felt in my heart that my dance with cancer was over. I had recovered. I didn't need a test to confirm it. My mom and I proceeded to host a fabulous victory party: a celebration of health and gratitude.

Two days after my party, my doctor called with the results of the cellular test: positive. Leukemic cells were still present in my marrow.

BUT HOW COULD THAT BE? I DID EVERYTHING RIGHT! AND I JUST PUT CLOSURE ON THIS WHOLE ORDEAL! WHAT THE #!@%* DID THIS MEAN?

My doctor was puzzled by the results and suggested the possibility of an error. He asked that I come in for another biopsy so they could rerun the tests at their original lab. I felt like it was starting all over again.

This time, it took me five full days to even peek out from my cloak of anger. I felt betrayed by my body, by my doctors and by the world. While I waited for the new results, I kept asking anyone who would listen, "HOW STRONG DO I HAVE TO BE?" I felt safest when I was curled up beneath the covers of my bed . . . no matter what time of day or night. Food was my drug of choice. Knowing better, I heard my own words echo in my mind: "Anger: feel it, deal with it, heal it." Like a tire spinning in thick mud, I was stuck in Step #1—I couldn't do anything but "feel it." . . . I knew this was okay. I trusted that I would move on to the other steps when I was ready, and eventually I did.

One very, very long week later, the new results came in: *No leukemic cells were apparent in my marrow.* The first lab had made a mistake. Thank goodness for second opinions! Thank God for healing! With a sudden jolt, the emotional roller coaster I was riding came to its final stop.

## KEY CONCEPTS: ACKNOWLEDGE ANGER

- It's okay to be angry.
- You are never upset for the reason you think you are.
- Overcoming anger requires you to feel it, deal with it and heal it.
- Set up time limits for your expression of angry feelings if you see that they could go on indefinitely.

## PUT IT TO PRACTICE: ANGER WORK SPACE

1. *What emotion* is at the base of my anger? Fear? Sadness? Guilt? Pain? Some other combination of emotions?

2. Accepting the idea that I am never upset for the reason I think I am, *what* am I so angry about?

3. *Why* is this so upsetting to me?

4. *How* will I effectively deal with this when I am ready?

5. When will I act on my above-listed options for dealing with this anger?

6. For future reference, some positive ways to express my anger include:

## *Thoughts and Notes*

*"When angry, count four; when very angry, swear."*
*–Mark Twain*

# RAGE PAGE

Write, scribble, tear the page out ... Start releasing the anger!

Let it out!

## *RACE TO WIN!*

Though I truly believe the journey is far more important than the destination, it's still good to know where we're headed. Early on, my friend Ian told me that I would survive this disease because I came from a family of "thoroughbreds." Not knowing exactly what that meant, but appreciating the horse analogy, I told him to bet all of his money on me because I intended to win the race. My goal was a complete remission and a long life. I decided that my metaphorical "horse's" name in this race for life would be *Michelle's Miracle.*

This name became symbolic to my family, my friends and me. We often referred to it when we were excited about my progress or when we needed some extra inspiration. My friend Claire even made me a *Michelle's Miracle* collage. She covered a piece of poster board with pictures of race horses and added positive affirmations from one of our favorite authors, Louise Hay. It was amazing! When I finished my chemotherapy treatments, I sent a *Michelle's Miracle* "press release" (see next page) along with a personal thank-you note to my all-star support team.

In the world of horse racing, races vary. Some are short; others are longer. Some take the form of a series (think "Triple Crown"), while others are one-time events. Horse names vary, too. People may bestow their horses with lucky names such as "Shiny Penny" or "Magic Hat," or perhaps choose family names such as "Hoshi's Habit" or "General Bartle." Some names are chosen because they're just plain fun or inspirational, like "Rise Above It," "On My Way to Greatness" or "Bring It On!"

- Embracing the race horse metaphor, what race is your horse running? Is it the race for a cure? Is it a race to a specific event or reunion? Is your goal to mend a relationship, hold your grandchild or be at peace with yourself? Identify your goal and go for it.
- What is the name of the horse that best represents YOU? What color is the horse? What color is the jockey wearing? Can you see yourself crossing that finish line? Get as specific as you can with your imagery, so that the picture you see in your minds' eye is unmistakable each and every time you view it.

**NAME YOUR HORSE, CHOOSE YOUR RACE . . . *AND WIN IT!***

## ANNOUNCE YOUR VICTORY

Choosing your race is a way of setting a clear goal in your mind. Achievement of that goal, whatever it may be, is cause for celebration. Again, paralleling the race horse metaphor, this was the actual announcement I sent to all of my friends and family when I received my clean bill of health:

### *"Michelle's Miracle" Takes First Place in the Race for Life!*

**THE ASSOCIATED PRESS**

SANTA CRUZ, CA The mighty thoroughbred, "Michelle's Miracle," ridden by first-time jockey Michelle Waters, recently won the race against leukemia. Said Waters of the victory, "It was a tough race with surprises and struggles at every curve. Still we endured, knowing that each step forward was well worth the effort." When asked about her phenomenal luck, Waters quickly answered that luck had nothing to do with it. "My success lies in my faith and my positive attitude, and continuous support from people who never stopped believing in me!"

## WHAT WILL YOUR ANNOUNCEMENT SAY?

LESSON

# 8

# Play the Part

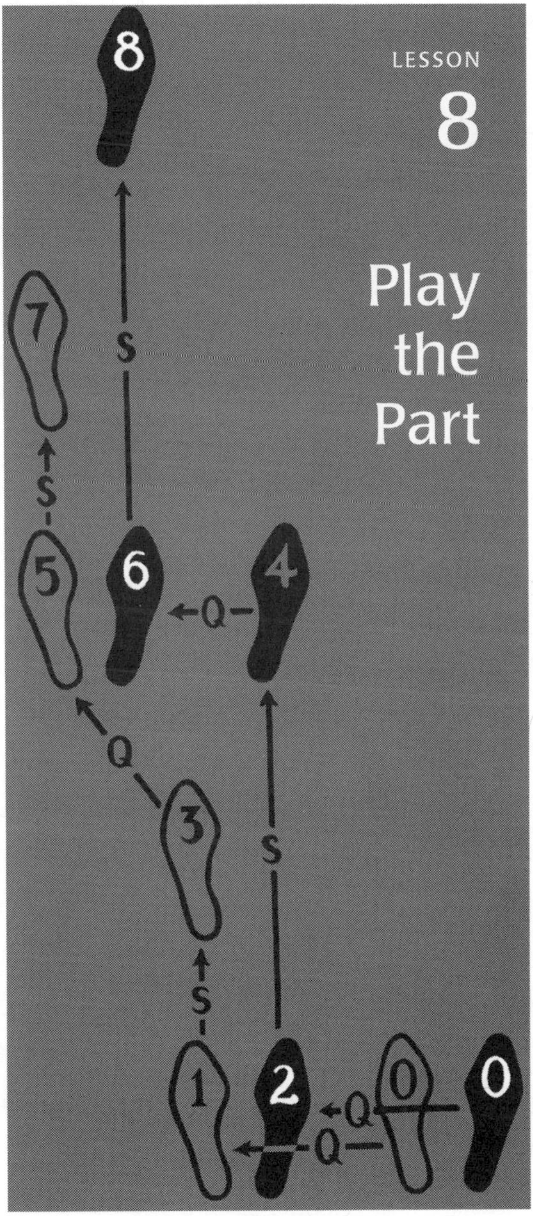

As we travel along the journey of life, our personalities become a tapestry of many different roles. Our family, employment and social ties influence these roles. Some are official; some are self-given. Typical roles might include parent, manager, significant other and so forth. We who face health challenges are constantly choosing new roles to try throughout our healing process. Here is a partial list of some of the roles I played during my dance:

| | |
|---|---|
| Student | Patient |
| Child | Writer |
| C.E.O. | Raging Lunatic |
| Teacher | Caregiver/Support Person |
| Wife/Lover | Communication Specialist |
| Optimist | Race Horse |

Though I traveled among many roles, each role was script-specific, having its own goal, rules and audience. In the role of the Child, I shamelessly and lovingly allowed others to take care of me. My wants and needs were explicit and expected to be met. I longed for my mother's comfort and often became scared. When I adopted the role of the Caregiver/Support Person, I calmed anyone close to me who might be hurting. I reassured my family and friends that I would be okay. I smiled whenever I could in order to ease other people's tensions. I spent hours on the phone soothing those shaken by the diagnosis. The Caregiver/Support Person role was the most exhilarating yet exhausting role for me.

Some roles served me well; others did not. In some stressful situations (typically when my husband Brian was the only one with me), I would slip into the Raging Lunatic role. Usually spurred by feelings of helplessness, the Raging Lunatic in me would perform Oscar-worthy temper tantrums over trivial things like the inability to find a certain lipstick!

After I started to pay attention to my different roles, I began to learn which ones best served me and which did not. I often felt the most optimistic when I was in the Caregiver/Support Person role, but least in control when I was in the Patient role. After careful examination, I learned to mix the roles. For example, when a concerned nurse came in to take my blood or vital signs, I purposely relayed one of my success stories to reassure her (and myself) that I was going to be just fine. I became skilled at jumping from my Patient role into my Caregiver role.

Because specific goals, scripts, audiences and rules accompany each role we take on, changing any one of those things ultimately affects the role. They are all interconnected. The role of Raging Lunatic and the goal "to let off steam" are compatible. However, the goal "to be at peace" would not be best met if its conduit was the role of Raging Lunatic. A closer look at our audience shows that obviously the role of Patient is compatible with an audience of a nurse, but look how effectively the role of Caregiver was for me when paired with that same audience. Changing your communication (your script and role) invariably changes the outcome of the situation. Be mindful of your options and creative in your pairings.

Exploring the different roles we play during challenging times like ours often helps explain why we act the way we do. Bringing these roles into our immediate consciousness also reminds us that we really do have control over our actions, words and thoughts. We can choose our roles. Choose the ones that work best for you!

## KEY CONCEPTS: PLAY THE PART

- We all have many different roles that we access for different situations.
- Each role comes with its own goal, script, rules and audience. Changing any one of these things ultimately affects the role.
- Identifying our roles and their subsequent goals and audience is a starting point for understanding our communication patterns and taking control of them.

## PUT IT TO PRACTICE

I strongly encourage you to discover the different roles you embody while dancing this dance. You can start by brainstorming a list of your roles. When you think you are finished, ask a close friend to see if there are any roles you may have overlooked. Along with looking at your family, work and social roles, know that your interests and hobbies point to specific roles, too. For instance, are you an online chatroom junkie? That may be one of your roles. Look it over: the role of

Chat-Room Junkie comes with its own script (a way of conversing in the chat rooms), its own rules (how to initiate a conversation, codes, etc.), its own audience (others online) and its own goal (social, fun). Who knows? That role may have a place in your healing. After listing your main roles, identify the goal and primary audience for each.

Example:

| Role | Goal | Audience |
|---|---|---|
| Student | To absorb knowledge and life lessons. | I use this role when I am mindful of my ability to learn from this disease. I have the opportunity to learn from doctors, other patients and all those around me. |
| Child | To feel nurtured and safe. | I often use this role in the presence of my mom. I sometimes fall into the role of the child with my spouse. |

When your list is complete, ask yourself the following questions:

1. Are your roles and goals compatible?

   *If not, how will you change them?*

2. Are your roles and audiences compatible?

   *Think outside the lines. Would any of these roles work with other audiences?*

3. Which roles empower you the most?

   *Can you adopt these roles more frequently?*

4. Which roles provide the most comfort in difficult times?

   *Can you call on these roles when necessary?*

5. Which roles could you stand to see less frequently?

   *Can you replace these roles with some of the others mentioned above?*

6. Are there any roles that you would like to adopt that aren't on your list?

   *Adopt them now!*

### *Thoughts and Notes*

*"To the man who only has one hammer,*
*everything he encounters begins to look like a nail."*
*—Abraham H. Maslow*

## SURROUND YOURSELF WITH THE POSITIVE. SHIELD YOURSELF FROM THE NEGATIVE.

- As a friendly reminder and icebreaker, post a colorful sign that reads: "Positive Energy Only Past This Point!" on your hospital room door or on your front door at home.
- When going in for a treatment, try to sit near a window. The options for fresh air and a view of the sky are revitalizing!
- Let those around you know that negative energy (whether in the form of a griping nurse or a groaning caregiver) has no place in your healing process.
- Remember to F.L.Y (Fully Love Yourself) through all situations. Positive energy starts with YOU!
- Cut out "lips" from models in magazine ads and tape them to your protective breathing mask (if you need to wear one). Count the number of smiles you inspire! It instantly puts others at ease and lets them know that even though they can't see your mouth, you're smiling anyway. Smiley-face stickers bring the same results.
- Take your favorite CDs (motivational or musical) and a portable CD player with a headset to treatment appointments and hospital stays.
- When applicable and possible, initially close the curtain that separates you from another patient who may be sharing the same treatment room. This not only gives each of you well-deserved privacy, but it protects you from any negativity that may come from the other side. Sadly, a positive disposition in the hospital is often the exception, not the norm. When you have had time to settle in and scope out your situation, you might choose to reopen the curtain and chat.
- Look for a miracle everyday. You'll find at least one, often more!

## LEARNING AND TEACHING JOURNAL PAGES

When I was first diagnosed, it was very clear to me that I had two distinct roles: I was to be a student of life and a teacher of it at the same time. Strangely enough, these roles were quite familiar to me, having been a graduate student and teaching associate at the time of my diagnosis. Still, as similar as these roles seemed, they were now so different because the subject matter that I was learning and teaching had changed so dramatically. While dancing with cancer, I knew I was to learn all I could about myself, my life and the people around me.

Whether it was a symposium about sunrises or a lecture on letting go, no lesson was too small and no subject was excluded. Simultaneously (and often unknowingly), I was called to teach others in the areas of strength, love and attitude.

Accepting this schoolroom metaphor for yourself, what kind of student are you? Are you sitting in the front of the class or are you busy doodling in the back? What kind of grades are you earning? Do you ask good questions? Do you do your homework? Do you work well with others?

When teaching, what kind of instructor are you? Are you understanding and empathetic or are you narrow-minded and self-righteous? Are you kind? Are you fair? Do you tailor your lessons to the students at hand? Do you push your students to be glorious, always seeing their potential? What is the theme of your curriculum?

Use the following pages to keep an accurate account of the lessons you are learning and the lessons you are teaching as you dance with the diagnosis.

**YOU ARE A STUDENT AND A TEACHER OF LIFE!**

**Lessons I am learning . . .**

**Lessons I am teaching . . .**

# Choose to Lead

You did not choose

to dance this dance,

but you can

choose to LEAD.

LESSON

# 9

# Experience Miracles Through Mindfulness

If I told you there is a way to improve the quality of your life, your relationships and your experiences with disease that costs no money and is available to you right now, would you be interested? If I said that you could become more aware, intuitive and peaceful by practicing this one method, would you read on?

Well, there is a way; there is a method. It's called *mindfulness*. Being mind*ful* is the opposite of being mind*less.* Mindfulness is the conscious presence with the moment. It is the awareness of the ocean's distant roar, the acknowledgement of a hungry stomach and the appreciation of a gardenia's sweet scent. It's also about being one with a bone-marrow transplant and sitting with the fear of the unknown. Instead of tuning into the "to-do" list in our heads, mindfulness allows us to stop and unite with the experience of the moment.

Mindfulness plays a very prominent role in our dance. Understandably, with disease we often focus on the future outcome at the expense of ignoring the present. How long will my treatments last? When can I go home? How long do I have to live? In some ways, keeping our eye on that future target helps us endure the challenge of today, yet there is still much to be gained from the now. After all, the present is all that we truly have, regardless of our prognoses. It's what really matters. Mindfulness reminds us of just that. As Sir Winston Churchill said, "It is a mistake to look too far ahead. Only one link in the chain of destiny can be handled at a time."

When in the hospital or clinic, mindfulness puts us in touch with the medical procedures we might normally ignore. When being mindful, the I.V. of antibiotics that drips into our veins (bringing promises of well-being) is not denied as we escape into the talk shows on the television. Instead, it is carefully studied. We are as one with it. We watch, perhaps in awe, as the liquid flows down its prerouted path. We notice the colors, the sound and the feel of this experience. We listen to our inner voice. What are we feeling? Is it fear? Anxiety? Gratitude? Peace? Are we experiencing any pain or discomfort? Where? How is our breathing? We inhale deeply, delivering oxygen to the tips of our toes. We are still. Mindfulness puts us in touch with the details of the moment.

We as Cancer Fighters know that tomorrow is uncertain and that today is what matters most. Louise Hay, author of *You Can Heal Your Life*, says, "The point of power is in the present." I love that! Our diagnoses reinforce this empowering mantra and give us the opportunity to slow down and see things for the first time again. For me, simple things like deep breathing and walking (things that had been taken away temporarily) seemed joyous and new when I practiced being mindful with them.

When my diet restrictions (due to chemotherapy) were removed, cantaloupe was one of the most delectable foods I had ever placed on my palate, thanks in part to being mindful. As I practiced being present, I didn't just taste the melon, I experienced it with all of my senses. I noticed that it was cool and a bit slippery. It was just soft enough to melt into my spoon as I silently scooped bite-sized slices. The cantaloupe's clean scent was stronger than I remembered and I salivated instantly upon the first whiff. I marveled at the melon's green and beige outer skin, contrasting it to the vibrant, colorful flesh of the inside. If painting, I'd need to blend dollops of orange, pink and white to come up with a color nearly as fresh as this one. As for taste, Willy Wonka himself would have sold his soul for the secret of this cantaloupe's perfect sweetness. Candy couldn't compare! Sticky trails of sugared juice marked my chin. For anyone else, this was probably an ordinary cantaloupe. For me, mindfulness made it magical!

To experience the power of mindfulness for yourself, try these simple steps.

1. Slow down. Feel yourself breathe: in . . . out . . . in . . . out . . . in . . . out, or listen to the steady beat of your heart. Do what it takes to get in tune with the here and now.

2. When you have centered yourself, make a mental note of your immediate external environment. What's going on around you? Where are you? Who is with you? Are you noticing anything new?

3. Access your senses. Calmly ask yourself what you are feeling, hearing, smelling, seeing and tasting. Describe these senses.

4. Look inward. What are you feeling inside? What emotions are present? What are you thinking? Be with these feelings.

5. If your mind begins to wander (and it most likely will), gently pull yourself back to the moment and continue.

Mindfulness is a wonderful way to fully experience the miracle of life without letting it go by too quickly and unnoticed. Meeting the present moment also reveals pathways to self-exploration and understanding.

Try tuning in when you are getting a treatment or getting angry. Be mindful when you are eating a meal or even washing the dishes. When communicating with others, avoid slipping into tired, worn-out communication patterns (automatic pilot) and be mindful instead. Notice the many alternatives you have in each communication interaction. Word choice, tone of voice and facial expressions are just a few of your options when you get centered and stay present. Being mindful in any moment opens avenues of choices and opportunities for control. If you are not present, where are you and why?

*Just for the record . . .* mindfulness might not work for you in all situations. Trust your instincts! I was not brave enough to practice the art of mindfulness with every one of my four bone-marrow biopsies. Sometimes staying present was the last thing I wanted to do. Instead of focusing on the moment during one particular biopsy, my husband told me stories of our first date and did whatever it took to take my mind far away from reality. Still, I am thankful for the times throughout my healing process when I did take the time to stop and smell the roses, so to speak. Truly, mindfulness makes the moment matter.

## KEY CONCEPTS: EXPERIENCE MIRACLES THROUGH MINDFULNESS

- Mindfulness is conscious awareness of the moment.
- Being mindful means tuning into the present, not the past or the future.
- Mindfulness requires slowing down and accessing our immediate surroundings, senses and emotions.
- When applied to communication, mindfulness illuminates choices.

## PUT IT TO PRACTICE

Try mindfulness *right now.* Go back to the five steps and try each one. For further appreciation of this art, give yourself a work week of mindfulness. Start by focusing on one of your five senses each day of the week. For example, dedicate Monday to the sense of sound. Pay special attention to what you hear on that day. Journal it. Make Tuesday about the sense of smell, Wednesday about taste, Thursday about sight and Friday about touch. Encourage your caregiver to take the journey with you. Marvel in what you had taken for granted. Celebrate the wonders you notice.

## *Thoughts and Notes*

*"How simple it is to see that we can only be happy now, and that there will never be a time that is not now."*

*—Gerald Jampolsky*

LESSON

# 10

# Emulate Others

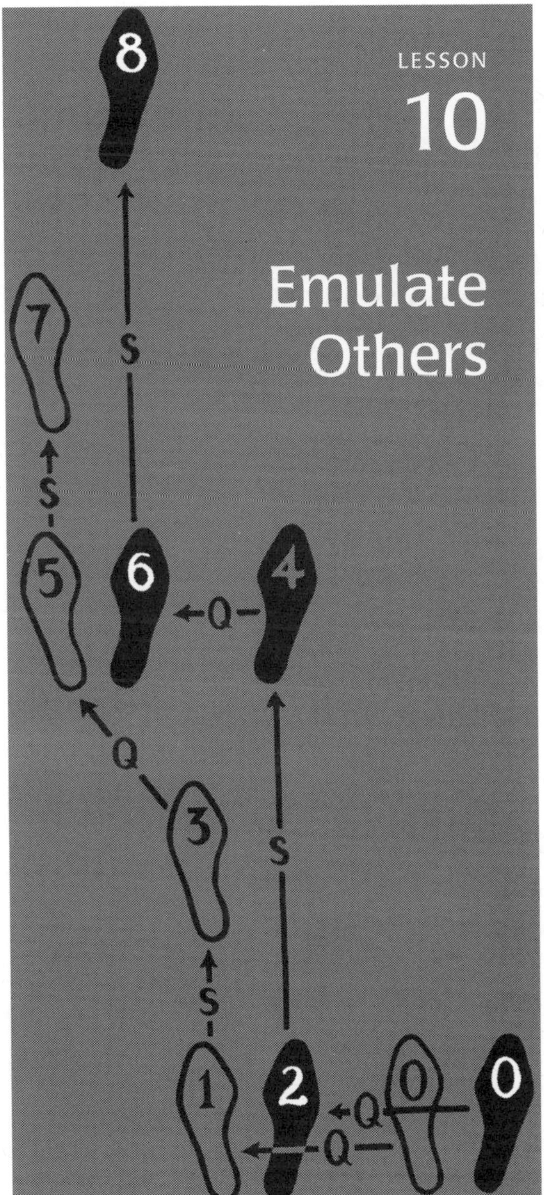

In one of my favorite movies, *A Fish Called Wanda,* Jamie Lee Curtis asks her not-so-bright partner in crime (the hilarious Kevin Kline) to think of a way out of a sticky situation. He is stumped for a solution, so Curtis cleverly asks him what one of his idols, the Greek philosopher Plato, would do if he found himself in the same predicament. The lights go on in Kline's mind and he figures out what must be done. Along with being quite funny, this scene demonstrates something we can do when we are stuck inside our minds and can't find our way out of stagnant thinking patterns. We can emulate, or try to be like, others whom we admire. What would our heroes do if they were fighting cancer? What attitude would those we most love and respect embrace? How can we be more like these people and mirror their positive characteristics?

When I first tried to do this, I listed five people I truly admire:

1. My mom
2. SARK (an inspirational author)
3. Dr. Robert H. Schuller (minister and founder of the Crystal Cathedral)
4. Oprah Winfrey
5. My dog Emi (okay, she's not exactly a "person," but I still admire her and learn from her all of the time)

Next, I imagined how they, *at their very best,* might handle a diagnosis of cancer:

1. My mom would not let others worry. She would keep smiling, she would never lose her will to live and she would be beautiful throughout the whole experience.

2. SARK cherishes emotions. She would embrace her tears and fears, then find a creative expression for them.

3. Dr. Schuller would dial his direct line to God, give thanks and keep a positive attitude. ("In all things be grateful!")

4. Oprah would educate herself and then others about the diagnosis. She would remain strong.

5. Emi, if she could comprehend disease, would do what she always does when she is not feeling well: she would take more naps, be very loving to herself and others, and would complain only when she really hurt.

After composing this list, I had a clearer picture of what was important to me and how I wanted to be. I valued my mom's *attitude*, SARK's *acceptance*, Dr. Schuller's *faith*, Oprah's *strength* and Emi's *unconditional love*. I felt inspired by some of my heroes and was encouraged to be more like them.

The key to emulating others is to *still be yourself* while adding new characteristics to your coping repertoire. This isn't about becoming someone new (although cancer certainly does have the power to transform us). Reflect on the positive people in your life. What examples do they set for you? Now is the time to put their lessons to use.

A simple alteration also makes this exercise work in the opposite way. For a quick reminder of how you *don't* want to behave through this experience, think of someone you *do not* admire. How might they handle your circumstances? If not conducive to your healing, stay as far away from emulating them as possible!

## KEY CONCEPTS: EMULATE OTHERS

- Another strategy for quick attitude and perspective shifts is to emulate positive characteristics of those we admire.
- The key to emulating others is to still be yourself while adding new characteristics to your coping repertoire.

## PUT IT TO PRACTICE: EMULATE OTHERS WORK SPACE

These are some of the people I admire:

1.

2.

3.

4.

5.

When at their best, here's how they might handle a situation like mine:

1.

2.

3.

4.

5.

Qualities of theirs I would most like to emulate are:

Ways I will try to be more like them include:

## *Thoughts and Notes*

*"People seldom improve when they have no other model but themselves to copy."*
*—Oliver Goldsmith*

## BADGES OF HONOR

A rare reaction to some medication I was taking resulted in very painful sores on my legs. A dermatologist took a biopsy of one of these and a small, yet noticeable, scar on the front of my right thigh was left behind. I showed the scar to Suzi, one of my ultra-optimistic friends.

"COOL!" she exclaimed with delight.

Puzzled by her enthusiasm, I asked her what exactly was so "cool" about an ugly scar.

Without missing a beat, she told me that it was a **badge of honor** marking one of my successful battles. What a shift in perspective for me! I decided to look at all other scars I collected in the same wonderful way.

**Go to a tree.**

**Study its trunk and branches. Have birds pecked at it? Have squirrels clawed at it? Have humans carved in it or cut off branches? Has the wind or a fire altered it?**

**Notice its beauty. Notice its strength.**

**Much like the tree's telltale signs, your scars are your badges of honor. They tell an amazing story that begins with, "Once upon a time, there was an incredible SURVIVOR . . ."**

**Hug the tree! Hug yourself!**

**GIVE A HUG TO SOMEONE YOU LOVE**
**AND WHO LOVES YOU, TOO!**

LESSON

# 11

# Create Clear Communication With Your Caregivers and Support People

I can hear it already: Is it caregivers or caretakers? Aren't they the same as support people? Does it matter? Isn't it just semantics anyway? I understand the confusion, so please allow me to differentiate the two roles—caregivers and support people—which together make up the support team.

Picture a bull's eye of love and care. Support people are the larger, outer circle; caregivers are the smaller, inner circle and the bull's eye in the middle is YOU! In greater detail, support people comprise the peripheral circle of friends, family and co-workers that surrounds the person diagnosed with disease. Like interconnected links of love, they show their emotional support by visiting, calling, praying for and/or writing to their friend in need.

Caregivers are essentially primary support people. They make up the tighter, central ring that encircles their loved one. They are often involved in the emotional and physical intricacies of the disease. Caregivers are typically close family members or "best" friends of the person diagnosed. As for the difference between caregivers and caretakers, it might just be semantics, but which would you rather have: someone *giving* care or *taking* it? When we choose our words wisely, "caregiver" is more empowering.

We are not the only ones who feel a loss of control when the diagnosis is cancer. Caregivers and support people go through their own feelings of anger, helplessness and confusion. In a sense, they dance their own dance with the diagnosis. They want what is best for us, but often have trouble figuring out what that is and how to deliver it. Roles are reciprocal: sometimes they need our help as much as we need theirs.

I wrote the Caregiver Contract with these thoughts in mind, to clarify needs and ease initial tensions. Used early on, it also establishes some healthy communication ground rules for you and your support team. The top portion of the contract provides basic guidelines for positive support. For example, sometimes caregivers get so preoccupied providing for their loved one that they forget to take care of themselves. (Item #5 reminds them of this.) Often people forget the power of their body language and greet individuals in our circumstances with expressions of worry and fear. (Item #2 will nudge them in the right direction.)

The bottom portion of the contract—our agreement—reminds us of our own commitment. For example, if we expect others to "never give up" (Item #7 of the top portion), then we'd better be willing to make the same promise (Item #1 of the bottom portion). This bottom portion holds us accountable. We are active participants in all parts of our healing process.

All guidelines were inspired by real experiences. If you like what it says, tear it out, copy it and give it to those you love. But don't just stop there. After you've given it to someone, *talk about it.* Remember that effective communication is something that happens *between* people. It is not a one-way event!

If some items don't pertain to you or you need to add others, please write your own Caregiver Contract. Start by brainstorming what you ideally want and need from your caregivers and support people. What could they do to help you emotionally, physically and spiritually? Do you need someone to let you vent when you feel frustrated, or even someone to promise to walk your dog twice a day? Don't be afraid to ask! If your requests are reasonable and will add to your peace of mind, then make them known. Your support team will likely appreciate the guidance.

Upon creating a list of your needs and wants, take a look at what your caregivers might need or want from you. Sure, they'll tell you they want nothing from you, but there are things you can do to help them through this time, too. (I know cancer can be all-consuming, but sometimes we need to get outside of ourselves and give to others.)

Whether or not your project turns into an actual "contract" is not as important as keeping the communication open between your caregivers and you. Honor this time of openness and don't be afraid to talk to each other.

## *Caregiver Contract*

1. Please do not be afraid of me. I am still the same person you've known and cared for; I just have a few new mountains to climb!
2. Please smile when you see me. Frowns bring me down!
3. Please ask me questions regarding my moods and feelings. It is not always correct to assume that I am sad, tired, mad or depressed. At times I might be, but other times I am experiencing feelings of peace, happiness and joy. Ask me how I feel and I'll tell you.
4. Please stay positive.
5. Please take very good care of yourself. You are extremely important to me.
6. Please gently ask my permission before trying to shift my perspective. Sometimes I am just not ready to look at the brighter side. I know you don't like to see me feeling low, but I need to travel through all my emotions instead of ignoring them. I'll let you know when I'm ready for a new perspective.
7. Please don't ever give up!

## *If you agree to the above, I, in turn, agree that . . .*

1. I will never give up.
2. I will be open and honest regarding my feelings (as soon as I know what they are).
3. I will be an active participant in my healing process. When agreed upon, I will follow my doctors' orders and I will maintain a healthy mental attitude.
4. I will tell you my needs and attentively listen to yours.
5. I will keep my sense of humor.
6. I will practice clear communication with you.
7. I will always appreciate your love and support.

## KEY CONCEPTS: CREATE CLEAR COMMUNICATION WITH YOUR CAREGIVERS AND SUPPORT PEOPLE

- Both caregivers and support people work together to make up a patient's support team.
- Caregivers involve themselves with the daily intricacies of the disease and care; support people work on the periphery, offering encouragement by visiting, calling, praying for and/or writing to their friend in need.
- Caregivers and support people benefit immensely from your clear communication.
- The Caregiver Contract makes communication explicit by highlighting your needs and wants throughout your dance with the diagnosis.

## PUT IT TO PRACTICE

Open up the channels of communication between you and your caregivers. What do you really need from those who surround you? What do they need from you? Begin by thinking in terms of emotional, spiritual and physical needs. Jot down some ideas below. Don't worry if the categories overlap (they often do!). They are just starting points for exploration. The bottom line is that it is easier to communicate when your desires are specific.

- **Emotional** (support, hope, perspective shifts, shoulders to lean on, reassurance, safety, humor, praise, encouragement, suggestions, optimism, time alone, fun, setting positive goals and celebrating accomplishments):

  **My Needs and Wants:**

  **My Caregivers' Needs and Wants:**

- **Spiritual** (prayers, affirmations, positive energy and attitudes, balance, inspiration, Scripture references, reminders of everyday miracles, tapes from church, meditation time, good books, aromatherapy, candles)

  **My Needs and Wants:**

  **My Caregivers' Needs and Wants:**

- **Physical** (errands, housekeeping, general assistance, walks, transportation, soft pillows and sheets, a pet sitter, great music, video rentals, healthy food, tasty treats, addressing thank-you cards, exercise, rest)

  **My Needs and Wants:**

  **My Caregivers' Needs and Wants:**

## *Thoughts and Notes*

*"Good communication is stimulating as black coffee and just as hard to sleep after."*
*—Anne Morrow Lindbergh*

# Be Grateful

Give thanks

for the healing

that is already

taking place.

LESSON

# 12

# Learn to Listen (Tips for Caregivers and Support People)

Though I strongly believe that all people need effective listening skills, this chapter targets caregivers and support people. As I traveled on my path with cancer, I often talked to those on my support team about how the disease specifically affected *them*. One recurring dichotomy in our discussions was their desire to make things better for me, coupled with the frustration of not knowing what to do. Those in the support roles frequently equate themselves with mechanics who need to fix the one who's hurting. In reality, the one who is hurting doesn't need to be "fixed" by their support team as much as they need to be *heard* by them. Many of my family members and friends didn't have to do much more than really listen to me in order to lift my spirits when I was feeling blue.

*Just listen.* Sounds easy, right? Well, it is . . . sort of. Listening is easy once we pay attention and commit to the practice of appropriate skills. As you probably know, listening involves much more than merely hearing what is said or staying quiet while another takes her[1] turn to speak. Effective listening starts with mindfulness (see Lesson 9). It begins by being present in the communication situation. The focus is on the moment. As good listeners, our thoughts are on the speaker's words and feelings instead of on our next response. Other common blocks to effective listening include daydreaming and judging the speaker's message as she delivers it.

1. To make this chapter easier to follow, I have used the example of a female speaker, thus using female pronouns. This replaces the cumbersome (yet accurate) "s/he" and "his-or-her" writing style. I hope it helps. Of course, good listening skills are applicable to both sexes.

**Active listening**[2] is a specific type of listening that allows the listeners to check their understanding of a speaker's verbal message (what she said) and nonverbal message (what she indicated through facial expressions, tone of voice and body language). Active listeners respect the speaker's ideas and feelings while encouraging her to explore those feelings further. (For the purposes of this chapter, the "speaker" is the person diagnosed with cancer; the "listener" is someone from her support team.) Active listening is particularly appropriate when someone is expressing negative feelings about something. Consider the following interaction:

**Speaker:** I am so sick of feeling sick. I'm not getting chemotherapy anymore!

**Listener 1:** You want to get better, don't you?

**Listener 2:** Imagine all the people whose treatments are lengthier and harsher than yours.

**Listener 3:** Chemotherapy is really a blessing. Twenty-five years ago, it wasn't even an option and people's prognoses were much worse. You're actually lucky to be getting it.

**Listener 4:** Don't talk like that! Don't you have any idea how much you mean to your family and me? This is hard for all of us!

---

2. Thomas Gordon developed the term "active listening" in 1975.

Hmmm . . . do you think that the speaker really feels "heard" by any of those listeners? Probably not. Each response is a well-intended attempt to change the speaker's perspective (an attempt to "fix it"), but each comes at the cost of denying the speaker's verbal and nonverbal message. As exemplified here, more communication is not always best. There is a time to listen. Active listeners tune into the speaker's message and then ask themselves, "What's really going on here?" Next, they check their perception of the situation by paraphrasing the speaker's statement with their interpretations of its meaning.

For example:

**Speaker:** I am so sick of feeling sick. I am not getting chemotherapy anymore!

**Active Listener:** You sound so upset. These treatments must be really rough on you.

Active listening involves empathy, or putting yourself in the speaker's position. It does *not* require agreement with what the speaker says, but it *does* necessitate a clear comprehension of the message as the speaker intended it. When paraphrasing the perceived meaning of what the speaker said, the active listener gets a chance to check if she understood the message correctly (the verbal words and the nonverbal feelings or intent) while leaving the floor open for the speaker to continue with her expression of emotion. Without words, the listener is saying, "I understand what you are saying and feeling. It is safe for you to tell me more." The speaker can make any correction in interpretation at this point.

### *Steps for Active Listening*

1. **Stay present.** Drop what you are doing or thinking and really *listen* to the speaker. Active listening requires putting your own "stuff" (i.e., worries, defenses, arguments) on hold. Don't worry: you can go back to your "stuff" later.

2. **Paraphrase.** After the speaker has spoken, paraphrase your interpretation of the message. Focus on both the actual words and the underlying feelings expressed in the message. What did you hear the speaker say? Repeat it in your own words. From this message and the way it was said, how do you think the speaker is feeling? Ask if your guess is correct. Remember that paraphrasing confirms you are hearing what the speaker has intended for you to hear and that the speaker is saying what she intended to say.

   **Precaution:** Avoid overusing phrases such as, "It sounds like . . ." or "I'm hearing you say that . . ." Liberal use of these phrases may make you sound mechanical and too much like a robotic therapist, not a caring friend. Use your own words and be as natural as possible.

3. **Monitor nonverbal language (both yours and theirs).** The nonverbal (body) language that accompanies active listening includes direct eye contact (natural, not staring), movement such as nodding your head (often indicating comprehension, not necessarily agreement) and use of phrases such as "uh-huh" that encourage the speaker to continue while indicating that you are following along. A good listener also monitors the speaker's nonverbal cues and looks for incongruities between the spoken word and conveyed meaning and feelings.

4. **Ask good questions.** Active listening involves asking questions that clarify terms ("What do you mean by that?"), elicit more information and aid in understanding ("Could you give me an example?") or encourage further discussion and subject exploration ("When is it the worst? When is it the best?"). Listeners may also use questions to help the speaker find her own resolution to the problem ("Ideally, how do you see this turning out?"). The power question, "What is *right*?" (or perhaps, "What *isn't* wrong?") can rescue your friend from a downward spiral of depression when asked with appropriate concern and matching nonverbal cues. In general, ask open-ended questions that prompt a speaker to elaborate, instead of closed-ended questions that require only a yes or no response.

5. **When permitted, reframe.** After the speaker has had ample time to vent, ask if she would like a different perspective (reframe). *If ready for reframing,* offer a new, healthier vantage point. *If your friend is not ready to shift perspective,* save it for a time when she is ready and willing to listen.

### *Sample Dialogue Using Active Listening*

**Speaker:** (1) I am so sick of feeling sick. I'm not getting chemotherapy anymore!

**Active Listener:** (2) You sound so upset. These treatments must be really rough on you. *(paraphrase content and interpreted feelings)*

**Speaker:** (3) They are! It's like the treatment is worse than the actual disease! I really didn't feel bad until I started chemo. I just want to feel well . . . and stay feeling that way.

**Active Listener:** (4) I bet you do. When will the treatments be finished? *(acknowledgement/question to elicit more information)*

**Speaker:** (5) Not soon enough.

**Active Listener:** (6) I can tell you've had it. What other options do you have? *(paraphrase interpreted feelings/question to find resolution)*

**Speaker:** (7) I guess I could just stop getting chemotherapy . . .

**Active Listener:** (8) Uh-huh . . . *(show that you're listening, while encouraging the speaker to continue)*

**Speaker:** (9) *(spoken softly)* . . . but then I increase my risks for a relapse.

**Active Listener:** (10) That sounds like a risk you're not willing to take. Can I offer a different perspective? *(paraphrase interpreted feelings/ask permission to reframe)*

**Speaker:** (11) I guess.

**Active Listener:** (12) I think the long-term benefits of chemotherapy ultimately outweigh the short-term hardships. Maybe we can talk to the doctors about different things you can do to ease the pain as you go through it . . . *(reframe)*

**Speaker:** (13) Yeah, at this point I'm willing to do just about anything . . .

As you can see from the example, the active listener allowed the speaker to explore her feelings before moving to the point of resolution. If the listener had reframed (Line 12) as soon as the speaker made her initial complaint (Line 1), the speaker may have become even more frustrated than before. She would be left to defend, explain or justify her position. Instead, the listener has encouraged the speaker to continue. The question posed in Line 6 pointed the speaker to her own resolution. This is good because, in situations such as this, a decision made by one's self is often more likely to be followed than a decision spelled out by someone else.

The practice of active listening is not a panacea; it is a needed skill, particularly when performing the support role. Most people who are diagnosed with a life-threatening illness need to be heard, not stifled or fixed. The support team that uses these skills benefits by creating a comfortable communication climate for their friends or loved ones in which they can vent frustrations. People on the receiving end of active listening techniques benefit by having a safe place to express their thoughts and feelings. When used appropriately, active listening is a win-win situation for all.

## KEY CONCEPTS: LEARN TO LISTEN (TIPS FOR CAREGIVERS AND SUPPORT PEOPLE)

- There is a time to listen.
- Active listening allows listeners to check their understanding of the speaker's verbal and nonverbal messages.
- Active listeners do not immediately judge, reframe or contradict a speaker's message (even if that's what they want to do). Instead, they listen carefully to what is being said and they encourage the speaker to continue.
- The steps to active listening include the following:

1. Stay present.
2. Paraphrase.
3. Monitor nonverbal language (yours and theirs).
4. Ask good questions.
5. When permitted, reframe.

## PUT IT TO PRACTICE

This exercise helps you assess where you're at and where you want to go with regard to listening skills.

1. Monitor your listening skills for the next 24 hours. Don't try to change anything; instead, simply notice how you listen. While doing so, keep the following questions in mind: Do you spend more time as a speaker or a listener? Do you formulate your next thought while the speaker is talking? Are there appropriate spaces in the conversation for you to gather more information and process what is said? What kind of nonverbal messages do you send when listening? (Check your posture, facial expressions, eye contact and distance from the speaker.) Are some people easier to listen to than others? Why? When is it most difficult for you to listen?

2. Spend 24 hours monitoring how others listen to you. Do you feel heard? Why or why not?

3. Make a plan to improve your listening skills. For lasting results, try to improve one specific thing at a time, adding others only when you feel competent with the previous one. Becoming a good listener is a skill that takes time and commitment.

   **I will improve my listening skills with** *(name)*

   ______________________________

   **by** *(pick one step such as "stay present" or "ask good questions")*

   ______________________________

   **I will know I have improved because/when** *(identify a noticeable outcome such as positive feedback from the named person or clearer comprehension of their situation)*

   ______________________________

## *Thoughts and Notes*

*"One friend, one person who is truly understanding,
who takes the trouble to listen to us as we consider a problem,
can change our whole outlook on the world."*
*—Dr. E. H. Mayo*

## THOUGHTFUL THINGS CAREGIVERS AND SUPPORT PEOPLE CAN DO TO SHOW THEY CARE

- When you hear of your friend's diagnosis and you are at a loss for words, try saying something like this: "I don't really know what to say, but I want you to know that I am here for you in whatever way you may need me."
- Have friends, family members or co-workers write down funny or inspirational movie rentals. Present your friend-in-need with the list along with free video/DVD rental coupons. Offer to pick up the movies.
- Send a "thinking-of-you" card each week.
- Send flowers long after your friend has been diagnosed. You'd be amazed at how many people (and flowers) are there in the beginning, yet fade out in the middle of the healing process.
- Make a tape or burn a CD containing your favorite upbeat, motivational songs for your friend to listen to when times get tough. Send along a Walkman for hospital stays and treatments.
- Make and give "Care Coupons." Offer to walk the dog, clean the house, run errands or whatever.
- Plant a healing garden where your friend can see it. The life and tranquility of such a gift is inspirational. It will also remind your friend of the love and support that you provide.
- Give your friend a special book that has nothing to do with disease.
- Personalize your friend's hospital room with posters, personal photos and homemade cards.
- Give tapes of sermons from missed church services.
- Lend your friend a special token (a stone you've held close, a family pin or a stuffed animal that's always "been there" for you). Proclaim that you want it back only when your friend is well.
- Say "I love you" often and mean it.

# Post Script: Miracles Are Coming Your Way

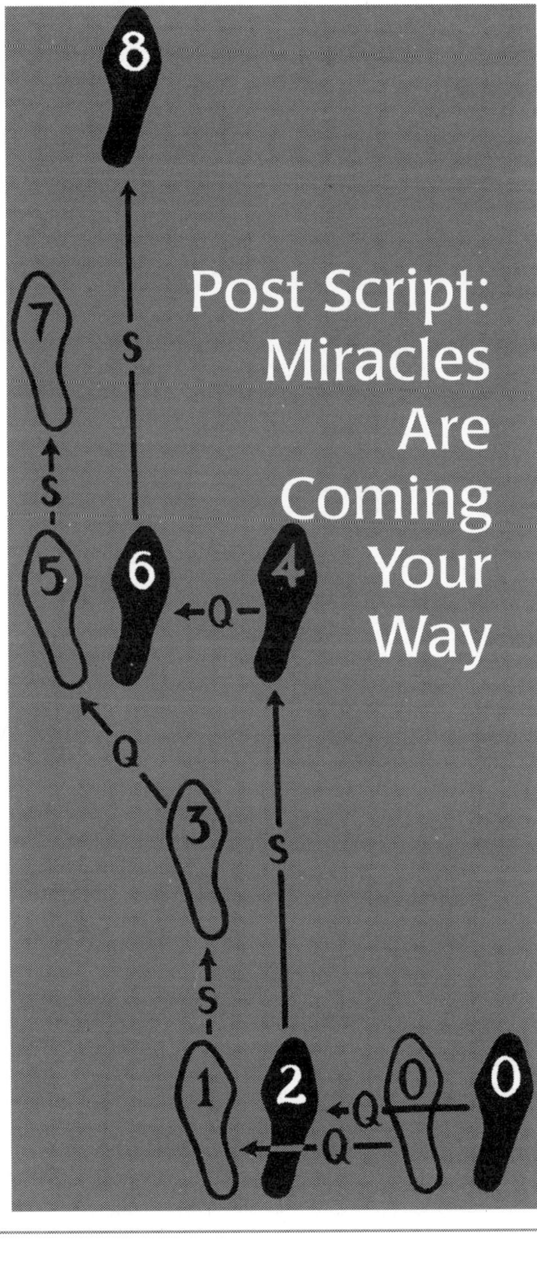

*The distance between Cancer and me increased.*
*We were back to back, barely touching,*
*and it was not long until his shadowy figure was just a blur.*
*As the song faded into the past, I found myself dancing solo.*

*I stopped . . . caught my breath . . . and smiled.*

*I slowly exited the dance floor a wiser and more beautiful person.*

I wrote most of this manuscript while I was still dancing with the diagnosis, meaning I was still undergoing treatments and experiencing the uncertainties of life associated with cancer. Today, my body is in remission—it has been for many years—and I have every intention of keeping it that way. I am dancing a new dance now, complete with new music, new moves and new partners.

I would say that my life is back to normal, but it will never be the same as it was before I was diagnosed with leukemia. As I see it, there are two distinct Michelles: the Pre-Diagnosis Michelle and the Post-Diagnosis Michelle. Which do I prefer? The Post-Diagnosis Michelle, without a doubt. Cancer, as terrible as it can be, was a great teacher to me. I learned about my values and myself. Thanks to cancer, I reorganized my thoughts and priorities. Each day, I try to live the life I have always wanted to live.

The tools I advocate in this book keep working for me today. I still recognize the power of language and I try to choose my words wisely. I never say that cancer is something I "had," but instead say it is something I "conquered." With regard to perspective, reminding myself that

I have a choice to see things differently is now second nature. It's just a part of who I am and how I think. I try to reframe everything—from interpersonal arguments to financial hardships (though sometimes those two are one and the same).

I choose assertive communication over passive and aggressive approaches whenever I am mindful of the option. At times I still struggle with self-acceptance, but not nearly as much as the Pre-Diagnosis Michelle did. When I fall into old patterns of self-degradation, I visualize how well my body worked for me when my life most depended on it. Today, I am much more respectful of my body than critical of it. Sometimes I stumble, but I now have many more steps in my repertoire to help me through tough times. Yes, I am dancing a new dance now, with new partners, too. Today I am dancing with Life, with Love, with Acceptance and with God.

In many ways, the transition out of disease is almost as difficult as the initial diagnosis. Disease can be all-consuming. For eight concentrated months of my life, I lived and breathed leukemia. As optimistic as I was about my recovery, I was not always certain it would happen. Then, with the last bone-marrow biopsy and my doctor's congratulations, it was over . . . almost as abruptly as it had started.

My calendar was free from daily doctor appointments and I experienced consecutive weeks of feeling well. My veins healed. My hair grew. The phone stopped ringing off the hook. As wonderful as it was, healthy living was somewhat foreign to me. I had trouble structuring my time and jumping back into the mainstream. Physically, I was fine; emotionally, I was standing in awe of what I had just been through.

Because I was diagnosed with leukemia just as I was finishing graduate school, I did not have a steady job to return to when I recovered. I had lots of time on my hands but didn't know how to organize it without a bevy of appointments and treatments. To help me get back on track, my mom matched me with a personal life coach.

My coach had nothing to do with working out at the gym. Instead, she helped me define and meet my goals by gently holding me accountable. I met with her on the phone once a week for three months and I made great progress. For me, having a coach was a much better choice than having a counselor. Though we did spend some time discussing emotional issues, we focused mostly on forward movement and organization. She helped me adjust to my new life.

With my family's full support, I also spent a fair amount of time processing my feelings. I wrote in my journal, read and spent lots of time with Emi, my dog. (Sometimes pets are the only ones who understand!) I acknowledged the enormity of my experience, put it to rest and moved on—and was better because of it.

I have moved past my diagnosis and subsequent treatment, but I am still committed to helping people in, through and out of a diagnosis of cancer. I volunteer for several cancer organizations, periodically visit leukemia support groups (so I can give support) and keep in touch with newly diagnosed people through the Internet. Staying involved with cancer keeps me present, centered and humble. I don't dwell on the past; I thrive on the present.

Though grateful for my experiences, surviving cancer is not the most amazing part of my life. My daughter is. My doctors weren't sure if I could have children but gave me the go-ahead to try. With lots of prayer, patience and persistence, I finally conceived in the fall of 2000 and gave birth to a healthy, beautiful baby girl in June 2001.

Brian and I named her Macy. The letters of her name, when paired with the first initial of her last name ("W" for Waters), stand for **M**iracles **A**re **C**oming **Y**our **W**ay. Nothing could be truer! She epitomizes hope, health and happiness. With her untarnished optimism and sparkling love of life, Macy reminds me not to take anything for granted. She unknowingly reinforces many of the lessons I learned while dancing with the diagnosis.

My challenge to you is to move beyond your own diagnosis. Make the Post-Diagnosis You better than the Pre-Diagnosis You. Dare to find good in the bad. Mend old ways, reprioritize and take this opportunity to make every moment count. Be a miracle, not a martyr.

Taking this journey with cancer is painful, heartbreaking and exhausting. It is also eye-opening and life-changing. Make cancer change your life for the better.

Dance that dance . . . and **always remember to lead**.

You Are Amazing!

Be a miracle

not a martyr.

The following list contains many empowering books, some of which are mentioned in the text. Covered topics include acceptance, attitude, cancer, communication and wellness.

- *Tuesdays With Morrie* by Mitch Albom (Doubleday, 1997)
- *The Cancer Conqueror: An incredible journey to wellness* by Greg Anderson, Abigail Van Buren (Turning Point Communications, 2000)
- *When Life Becomes Precious: A guide for loved ones and friends of cancer patients* by Elise NeeDell Babcock (Bantam Books, 1997)
- *Living, Loving, Learning* by Leo F. Buscaglia (Fawcett Books, April 1990)
- *Chicken Soup for the Surviving Soul: 101 healing stories to comfort cancer patients and their loved ones* by Jack Canfield (editor), Mark Victor Hansen, Patty Aubrey, Beverly Katherine Kirkhart and Nancy Mitchell-Autio (Health Communications, Inc. (HCI), 1996)
- *Taming Your Gremlin: A surprisingly simple method for getting out of your own way* by Rick Carson (Quill, 2003)
- *The Dragon Doesn't Live Here Anymore: Loving Fully, Living Freely* by Alan Cohen (Fawcett Books, 1993)
- *There's No Place Like Hope: A guide to beating cancer in mind-sized bites: A book of hope, help and inspiration for cancer patients and their families* by Vickie Girard, Dan Zadra (editor) (Compendium. 2001)
- *Peace is Every Step: The Path of Mindfulness in Everyday Life* by Thich Nhat Hanh, Arnold Kotler (editor) (Bantam Books, 1992)
- *You Can Heal Your Life* by Louise L. Hay (Hay House, 1999)

- *Love is Letting Go of Fear* by Gerald G. Jampolsky, Hugh Prather, Jack Keeler (illustrator) (Celestial Arts, 1988)
- *Full Catastrophe Living: Using the wisdom of your body and mind to face stress, pain and illness* by Jon Kabat-Zinn, Thich Nhat Hanh (preface), Joan Borysenko (Delta, 1990)
- *Anatomy of the Spirit: The seven stages of power and healing* by Caroline Myss, Ph.D. (Random House 1997)
- *The Power of Positive Thinking* by Dr. Norman Vincent Peale (Ballantine Books, 1996)
- *Succulent Wild Woman* by Sark (Fireside, 1997)
- *Tough Times Never Last, But Tough People Do!* by Dr. Robert H. Schuller (Bantam Books, 1984)
- *Fierce Conversations: Achieving Success at Work and in Life, One Conversation at a Time* by Susan Scott (Viking Penguin, 2002)
- *The Survivor Personality: Why Some People are Stronger, Smarter and More Skillful at Handling Life's Difficulties . . . and How You Can Be Too* by Al Siebert, Ph.D. (Berkley Publishing Group, 1996)
- *Peace, Love and Healing: Bodymind Communication and the Path of Self Healing: An Exploration* by Bernie S. Siegel, M.D. (Perennial Press, 1998)
- *A Return to Love: Reflections on the principles of a Course in Miracles* by Marianne Williamson (Harper Collins, 1993)
- *A Course in Miracles By The Foundation of Inner Peace* (1975)

Michelle Waters is a dynamic presenter who brings her passion for empowering others through communication to every speaking engagement. You may arrange for her to speak with your group by contacting Rising Star Press.

Hear an inspirational message from the author and leave her a personal message in return by calling the *Dancing with the Diagnosis* encouragement line at 831-621-9515.


**Rising Star Press**

*Quality Books that Inform and Inspire*

Box 66378

Scotts Valley, CA 95067-6378

Phone: 888-777-2207

Fax: 831-461-0445

e-mail: editor@RisingStarPress.com

Visit us on the internet at

www.RisingStarPress.com

CPSIA information can be obtained
at www.ICGtesting.com
Printed in the USA
BVHW062312081021
618516BV00002B/46

9 781108 482745